# The Black Side of the River

# The Black Side of the River

Race, Language, and Belonging
in Washington, DC

Jessica A. Grieser

Georgetown University Press / Washington, DC

THE AREA OF WASHINGTON, DC, UNDER STUDY IN THIS
VOLUME IS SITUATED ENTIRELY ON LANDS WHICH BELONG TO
THE NACOTCHTANK PEOPLE AND THEIR DESCENDANTS, THE
PISCATAWAY CONOY PEOPLE.

Library of Congress Cataloging-in-Publication Data

Names: Grieser, Jessica A., author.
Title: The Black side of the river: race, language, and belonging in Washington, DC /
    Jessica A. Grieser.
Description: Washington, DC: Georgetown University Press, [2022] | Includes
    bibliographical references and index.
Identifiers: LCCN 2021005007 (print) | LCCN 2021005008 (ebook) | ISBN
    9781647121525 (hardcover) | ISBN 9781647121532 (ebook)
Subjects: LCSH: African Americans—Washington (D.C.)—History. | African
    Americans—Washington (D.C.)—Language. | Sociolinguistics—Washington
(D.C.) | Discourse analysis—Washington (D.C.) | Anacostia (Washington, D.C.)—History.
    | Washington (D.C.)—Race relations. | Washington (D.C.)—History.
Classification: LCC F202.A5 G75 2021 (print) | LCC F202.A5 (ebook) | DDC 975.3—dc23
LC record available at https://lccn.loc.gov/2021005007
LC ebook record available at https://lccn.loc.gov/2021005008

∞ This paper meets the requirements of ANSI/NISO Z39.48-1992
(Permanence of Paper).

23 22      9 8 7 6 5 4 3 2  First printing

Printed in the United States of America

Cover design by Amanda Hudson, Faceout Studio
Interior design by Paul Hotvedt

*For my parents*

# Contents

# Acknowledgments

No work of scholarship is ever created in a vacuum, even if it feels that way at times, and I owe a large debt to a number of people whose support in various forms sustained the ten-year endeavor which took this project from conception to completion. First, a thank you to the scholars who helped with the very inception of this project—my graduate school mentors, Natalie Schilling, Jennifer Nycz, and Sonja Lanehart—who all provided invaluable guidance on the beginning of this work, enabling me to grow as a scholar in ways that allowed me to realize the full potential of this project as it matured from the dissertation which started it.

Thank you to my editors, Clara Totten, Rachel McCarthy, and the team at Georgetown University Press, who saw this book for what it would be from the very beginning and helped me make it the book that it is. Thank you also to the three anonymous reviewers who provided invaluable feedback on two drafts.

The community of Black linguists welcomed me as a scholar with open arms and sustained me as I worked on this and other projects. This work has benefited from conversations at conferences, over dinners, and during phone calls with many of my Black linguist colleagues, especially John Baugh and John Rickford, Arthur Spears, and Tracey Weldon. I am a better scholar and a better person for their support and look forward to giving back to this ever-growing community.

Several peers and colleagues read chapters of this work as I went through revision rounds, and so I thank Jennifer Delfino, Mary Kohn, Katie Carmichael, Anne Curzan, and Sarah Croco for their feedback on various parts of this work at various times. This book also benefited from the careful reads and feedback provided by three anonymous reviewers, who, among other things, gave me the impetus I needed to truly transform the work into a piece of accessible, usable scholarship. I also enlisted the help of Kathleen Kearns in the developmental editing of a major revision of this work and I thank her for her careful editorial eye, guidance, and patience as I wrote and rewrote.

This work would also not exist were it not for my fellow academics, who kept me motivated during the writing: my graduate program writing group of Julie Lake, Amelia Tseng, Kaitlyn Tagarelli, and Laura West, and my daily accountability group of Sarah Croco, Leanne Powner, Michelle Allendorfer, Sarah Fischer, and Thomas Flores.

This project was supported by several grants at the University of Tennessee: the Hodges Research Grant, two undergraduate research grants, and a Chancellor's Grant. In addition to supporting my research, the grants supported the work of several talented graduate and undergraduate research assistants, Abby Lauerman, Katie Green, Elizabeth Sloop, and Peyton Ritchie, all of whom made valuable contributions to the project with their careful coding, transcription, and insightful questions. I also thank Sinae Lee, whose parallel work on Southeast DC provided some of the data used in this project and whose publications since then have provided additional challenges to my own conceptions of this place.

Robbie Brown's work on his blog, *ZGeography*, provided fantastic nuggets of information for me when considering DC's changing cultural geography. I thank him in particular for allowing me to freely reproduce his cartography in this book.

Thank you also to my parents, whom I promised I would write only one dissertation only to go back on that promise and write a book. They walked this road with me, and for the myriad ways the process was easier due to their support, I owe them.

Finally, the roots of this project stem from the highly socio-logical work I did on language and place with Deborah Schiffrin. While she became too ill too quickly to see even the dissertation version of this work come to fruition, her approaches to thinking about the role of discourse in creating senses of place underpin so much of my own.

This book argues above all else that there is no "place" without people. People are the ones who, through our own personhood and experiences, bring the physical world into being. I thank the people of Historic Anacostia who allowed me to interview them, sometimes more than once, and welcomed me into their homes and their lives with their stories and their thoughts. I hope that I have written a work that honors their experiences, does them justice, and invites others into the richness of this Black community on the river.

# "I Expected the Streets to Be Paved with Gold"

Anacostia and Washington, DC, in the Black Imagination

I've known rivers:
I've known rivers ancient as the world and older than the
    flow of human blood in human veins.
My soul has grown deep like the rivers.
    —Langston Hughes, "The Negro Speaks of Rivers"

In 1920, aboard a train hurtling over the Mississippi River, Langston Hughes was awed by the enormity of the body of water he was crossing. He remembered his grandmother telling him that to be sold down the Mississippi was the worst fate an enslaved Black person could meet, and he recalled that it had been the sight of this terrible trafficking in humans that had helped lead Abraham Lincoln to sign the Emancipation Proclamation. Rivers, Hughes understood, were integral to the African, and therefore African American, experience, and the poem he first drafted on that train ride and later published in *The Weary Blues* connects African American experience to African experience in the cradle of civilization in Mesopotamia.[1]

In my hometown of Cincinnati, the mighty Ohio River separates Kentucky, a slaveholding state, from Ohio, a free state. Slaves sneaked their way through the woods of eastern Kentucky to then wade, swim, or be smuggled by barge into Ohio, where they were granted freed status. The National Underground Railroad Freedom Center now stands on a symbolic location: the Cincinnati-side bank of that river where so many enslaved descendants of African peoples made the perilous crossing from bondage to freedom.[2]

Rivers continued to be part of the country's shift from enslavement to equality. When civil rights icon Dr. Martin Luther King Jr. led demonstrators across the Edmund Pettus Bridge in Selma, Alabama, on March 7, 1965—"Bloody Sunday"—armed police officers beat them back with clubs and tear gas. The demonstrators successfully crossed the bridge fourteen days later, and the televised images of the police assault roused and broadened support for African American voting rights.

When Black people cross rivers, it matters.

This is a book about Black people whose lives are defined by a river and who cross it. It is a book about what it means to be from one side of that river instead of from the other. It is a book about community and the way that the river can carry people and their history; the way that a river can form a boundary that protects even as it separates.

This is a book about a city, Washington, DC, which almost from the day of its inception provided unparalleled options for African Americans, even as it simultaneously served as one of the major places where enslaved people were moved like chattel. It is a book about how one river rather than another came to matter in a different way, and what that second river means to the people who live beyond it.

This is also a book about language. It is a book about the way language helps a community on one side of a river shape its experience. It is a book about how that same language shapes the way others understand that community's experience, their lives and their neighborhood. It is a book about the ways that language connects people to one another, to their land, and to their history.

Hughes titled his poem "The Negro Speaks of Rivers." For a Negro to speak of a river is to speak to the entire history of that river and the ways it intersects with the complicated lived history of Black Americans. This book explores what it means to speak of a river and the ways that language and its use are implicated for people who speak of one particular river: the Anacostia River in Washington, DC. On one side of that river a growing white population has changed the racial makeup of a city once dubbed "Chocolate City" because of its overwhelming African American population and the rich Black culture instantiated there. On the other side, the African American population has concentrated and watched as the city has changed and those changes have slowly crept into this last Black Washingtonian space. This is a book about the ways that language shapes the understanding of place, lays claim to place, and forms community in a place. And it is a book about the people who make up that place: Black Anacostians, the souls who have grown deep like their river.

**The Other River**

Washington is a location which by its very definition is a place of rivers. On July 9, 1790, Congress passed the Residence Act, which fulfilled the requirement set out by the 1788 Constitution: a parcel of land would be set aside for the creation of the seat of the new government of the United States of America. The choice of locale was a compromise to balance the creation of the new National Bank of the United States, which would centralize the country's economy in the Northeast and place the nation's capital in the South, in close proximity to the plantations of several of the Founding Fathers. [3]

The capital city was originally planned as a ten-mile square set on its edge, so that it appeared as a diamond on a north-south –oriented map. [4] It was to be made up of roughly equal parcels of land ceded by the then-fourteen-year-old states of Maryland and Virginia. [5] At that time, the area chosen to become the federal district encompassed several existing settlements, the largest of which were Alexandria, in the Commonwealth of Virginia, and

Georgetown, in the state of Maryland. For just over fifty years the federal district remained as the diamond-shaped parcel, and the new government erected buildings on the Maryland side of the Potomac River, building the White House in 1792 and the US Capitol Building in 1850.[6] The Potomac is often talked about as if it were Washington, DC,'s only river. Yet the Residence Act invokes not one but three rivers, declaring that "a district of territory . . . on the River Potomac, at some place *between the mouths of the Eastern Branch and Connogochegue*, be . . . accepted for the permanent seat of the government of the United States."[7]

The Eastern Branch River flows across the southernmost part of the state of Maryland, meeting the Potomac River where it divides Maryland from Virginia. In the beginning both the Potomac and the Eastern Branch were part of Washington, DC's territory. The diamond stretched north and south of the Potomac and east and west of the Eastern Branch. However, as tensions began to rise between the Northern and Southern states in conflicts that precipitated the US Civil War, the Commonwealth of Virginia, fueled by the District's ban on slavery and citing a changing tax basis and the lack of any federal buildings on its side of the Potomac, reclaimed its land.[8] The Virginia Retrocession Act of 1846 returned Alexandria to the Commonwealth, and although President Abraham Lincoln later tried unsuccessfully to reclaim these lands during the Civil War, ultimately only the land Maryland ceded remained.

The retrocession, and the rearrangement of Washington which resulted from it, changed the relative importance of the rivers. Washington, DC, became defined by the Potomac River, the sole divide between the capital and the land beyond.

But the Eastern Branch did not cease to matter. It too formed a divide, even if it was a divide between the western and eastern parts of the same city. The people on one side of the Eastern Branch crossed bridges to get into downtown Washington. As Washington developed and grew, increasingly the Eastern Branch came to separate affluence from poverty, crime from safety, and, importantly, whites from Blacks.

By the time Congress had officially moved to Washington in the early 1800s, the Native American name for this second river had already come to be in wide use.[9] The word *Annakastia* came to stand for this second river as well as for the part of Washington that lay east of it. Today, moving residence across the Potomac requires a new license plate and makes you subject to different taxes and different laws. But crossing the Anacostia is every bit as meaningful, as it takes you into the heart of DC as an African American place.

### Gainin' on Ya: Washington before 1970

"When I came to Washington, I expected the streets to be paved with gold," Mr. Moore says.[10] A resident of Historic Anacostia since he arrived in his early twenties, Mr. Moore, now in his seventies, is a regular participant in the neighborhood senior group that I interviewed in 2015. A native of North Carolina, Mr. Moore is one of the many African Americans who took part in the Great Migration of the twentieth century, when a large percentage of African Americans from southern states migrated to several urban centers in the north and west to escape oppressive Jim Crow laws and pursue opportunities in the factory and service economies that dominated the northern cities.[11] During his high school years Mr. Moore encountered a teacher who had been educated in Washington and who spurred his own desire to make the two-state move north:

> I had a professor, in the ninth grade. He was a mathematician, and he was an excellent excellent teacher. But he was a graduate of Howard University, and he talked about Howard University, and this was my first introduction to Howard University. He talked about Howard University as though it was heaven! I mean

he he talked about the intelligentsia, and the mass of degrees that that were conferred upon African Americans, and how they were taking over large cities in the world. And I– to listen to him talk because he was such a loved– he had such a love for Howard. I immediately put it in my mind: "I got to see this place. I got to go to school there. Got to know what it's about. Got to know what's happening."

Washington is often referred to as Chocolate City, a moniker the band Parliament-Funkadelic gave it in their 1975 hit song of the same name. The song, which begins, "They still call it the White House, but that's a temporary condition, too," imagines the federal government run by African Americans, with Muhammad Ali as president, Aretha Franklin as First Lady, and Stevie Wonder as Secretary of Fine Arts. It points to the overwhelming population of African Americans in the area at the time, claiming that "You don't need the bullet when you have the ballot." The lyric "Gainin' on ya," which is a refrain throughout the song, emphasizes the steady and seemingly irrepressible growth of the African American population the District has always been home to.[12]

Many members of this large and vibrant population have made indelible contributions to African American history and culture, beginning with a substantial free Black population at the time of the city's founding, which would go on to become majority free well before the start of the Civil War.[13] DC is the home of famous Black abolitionists Sojourner Truth and Frederick Douglass, political giants such as Thurgood Marshall and Colin Powell, poets Paul Laurence Dunbar and Langston Hughes, and musicians Duke Ellington and Marvin Gaye.[14] The District has long been recognized as a mecca for the Black middle and upper classes from across the United States who came to Washington in the 1940s, 1950s, and 1960s to take advantage of its economic opportunities. Howard University, a historically Black higher education institution, educated lawyers and doctors, among others, and some of them stayed in Washington and became the city's Black elite. Neighborhoods such as upper Sixteenth Street, known to many of the capital's African American residents as "the Gold Coast," were populated until the late twentieth century with many of the nations' wealthiest Blacks.

This pattern was mirrored in other cities such as Atlanta, New York, and Detroit.[15] The ways in which Black people changed the nature of and recharacterized the cities to which they moved is well documented in the fields of cultural geography and sociology. The "Chocolate Cities" framework, which draws its name from the same Parliament-Funkadelic song mentioned earlier, holds that the ways that Black Americans inhabit space and experience spatial mobility require us to think about the United States differently.[16] Instead of being a land that is separated into the discriminatory South and the welcoming North, as the classic racial narrative would have it, the Chocolate Cities framework draws on Malcolm X's infamous statement that "as long as you South of the Canadian border, you South."[17] We would better think of the United States as multiple "Souths," the framework argues: a country where regional identities are inextricable from the histories of the Black people who have moved through those spaces and who, in turn, informed the way those spaces are understood.

Washington is one such South. From its beginnings as a major slave-trading port in the seventeenth century, descendants of African slaves have always been a significant part of the city's makeup.[18] In the twentieth century, however, the presence of those descendants multiplied rapidly. During these years the racial makeup of Washington flipped, from a population that was approximately 30 percent African American in 1930 to its peak in 1970, when the District's 530,000 African American residents made up just over 70 percent of its population.[19] A major cause of this growth was the continued growth of opportunities for whites in other parts of the still-segregated United States. Because whites could find lucrative employment easily in the highly segregated, discriminatory private sector, jobs with the federal government attracted the incoming Black community.[20] The private sector jobs usually paid more than the government ones did, a disparity that ultimately drove both sides of the equation of DC's dramatic racial shift during these years—higher pay elsewhere meant that whites left the District, while the security of lower-paying federal jobs, where racial discrimination in hiring was also forbidden by law, meant plentiful opportunity for Black Washingtonians. As Washington headed toward the 1970s, it appeared that nothing would stop the continued growth of the African American population and their control of the city. But then, on one dark afternoon, all that momentum suddenly began to change.

### "Chocolate Melts": The Changing Landscape of Washington, DC

On the evening of April 4, 1968, horrifying news was spreading through radio, over television broadcasts, in newspaper special editions, and by word of mouth: civil rights activist and Black community lion Dr. Martin Luther King Jr. had been assassinated, shot to death in Memphis, Tennessee, by a then-unknown assassin who would turn out to be James Earl Ray. The civil rights movement, which had promised a new kind of freedom to Black Americans suffering under unjust Jim Crow laws in the South, and less codified but no less prejudicial discrimination in the North, had been taking deep root, and African Americans across the country benefited from increased voting rights, civil liberties, and access to newly integrated spaces. The assassination of King was a monumental backlash against the gains that had been made, and the nation's African American community reacted in horror, shock, and, finally, rage.

As news of the assassination spread, protesters from the Student Nonviolent Coordinating Committee (SNCC), along with their former leader, Stokely Carmichael, gathered at the corner of Thirteenth and U Streets in DC's Northwest Quadrant to demand that stores in the neighborhood close out of respect. As the evening went on, the crowd of protestors grew increasingly larger and some members eventually became violent and began looting.[21] Although DC Mayor-Commissioner Walter Washington called for the damage to be cleaned up later in the evening, protests the following day after a rally Carmichael led at Howard University led to violent clashes with the Washington Metropolitan Police Department in the areas of Seventh Street NW and H Street NE, eventually resulting in arson attacks on several buildings and protesters blocking firefighters from responding to the fires.[22] In the end President Lyndon B. Johnson chose to mobilize thirteen thousand national guard troops to restabilize the city, but not before entire areas of the neighborhoods of U Street, Columbia Heights, and H Street NE were left in rubble. In the end, thirteen lives were lost, and the destruction, concentrated entirely in DC's most thriving Black communities, diminished the prosperity of those communities for decades to come.[23] Over the course of the next several years more than 40 percent of the 909 businesses that were affected directly by the riots closed and others struggled on into the 1970s but ultimately did not make it.[24]

The larger effect of the riots, however, was not seen in the economic opportunities of the business owners and their patrons but rather in the racial demographics of the District. By 1968, affluent white District residents had already begun to flee for neighboring counties in Maryland and Virginia, leading to the sharp rise in the African American population which characterized the 1960s. The riots changed the African American population too. The riots, and the ensuing divestment of social and economic capital from the once-vibrant Black communities in the city, meant that the Black middle-class, the educated "intelligentsia" that Mr. Moore came to seek, began to make their exit as well. Tana, a forty-four-year-old woman who attended the Barry Farm preschool in Historic Anacostia in the early 1970s, remembers the exodus marked this time in her childhood: "I think there were certain age groups of people that were staying. Like older people were staying but younger people with children were moving to Maryland. That was the big thing. You know, 'We're moving to Maryland. We're moving to Maryland. We're moving to Maryland.'"[25]

The refrain "We're moving to Maryland" captures the direction of egress for the Black Washingtonians. Washington, DC, is surrounded by a number of suburbs, many of which serve as home to the region's hundreds of thousands of federal government employees. To the northwest, Washington is bordered by Montgomery County, and to the east and south by Prince George's (PG) County, both in Maryland. Across the Potomac River, Arlington County, Virginia, is made up of the land that was part of Washington, DC, until the Virginia retrocession. To DC's African Americans, the promise of a solid pension-paying government job was a reason to come to Washington in the first place, and so to leave DC and its connection to Black culture and community was out of the question. So they moved just over the borderlines of Southern and Eastern Avenues into PG County.[26]

White DC residents, who had already been leaving the city in droves, went in a different direction—across the Potomac River, to Arlington and Fairfax Counties. This led to a racially bifurcated settlement pattern in the adjacent counties: DC's former white residents overwhelmingly emigrated to Virginia and, to a lesser extent, Montgomery County, while DC's Black residents predominately moved to PG County. There are several probable reasons for this pattern. 1968 was only a little more than a decade after the official abolishment of Jim Crow laws in the south, which included Virginia. As such, there remained a greater hostility to African American residents in the Virginia suburbs than in Maryland. A federally funded study that was reported in the *Washington Post* in 1986 presented area landlords with fictitious prospective renters matched for income and background but not for race.[27] Although landlords across the board preferred prospective renters who were white, landlords in northern Virginia in particular chose white renters 12 percent more often than did landlords in PG County, which was also the only county adjacent to DC where the landlords showed a less-than-50-percent preference for white residents.

Besides PG County being friendlier to Black residents, another possible explanation for the racial pattern lies in the county's geography with respect to the District.[28] When French architect and Revolutionary War hero Pierre L'Enfant was asked to draw up the city plan in 1791, he created a city on the order of the great European cities at the time, superimposing wide diagonal avenues over a gridded street system.[29] Instead of organizing the city around the home of a monarch, however, L'Enfant emphasized the democratic rule of the new nation: the Capitol Building, which was to house the two chambers of Congress, was placed at the highest point of the city. Two streets, one north-south and one east-west, but both named Capitol Street, intersect at the Capitol's grounds and separate the District into four quadrants: Northwest (NW), Northeast (NE), Southwest (SW), and Southeast (SE). As a result, any street or address within the grid must have its place within the quadrant specified: crossing Capitol Street traveling south will change the name of the street you are driving on from Seventh Street NW to Seventh Street SW, and any given address may be duplicated as many as four times across the city. Even the most famous address in Washington is subject to this quadrant-driven repetition: 1600 Pennsylvania SE is an apartment complex which opened in 2015 in the Capitol Hill neighborhood, sixteen blocks east of Capitol Street, whereas the home of the US president sits sixteen blocks to the west of the divide.[30]

Over the decades Washington, DC, has developed a distinctive racial pattern across the four quadrants, such that the District's white residents tend to reside in the north and west and its Black residents tend to reside in the south and east.[31] PG County immediately abuts the Northeast and Southeast Quadrants, the two areas of the District that have historically been home to the highest concentrations of Black residents. Moving to Prince George's County, therefore, gives Black residents easy access to their friends, family, and churches in the District.

Post-1968 these movements of both Black and white residents characterized the exodus from the city, ultimately causing many of the professional class of all races to move outside the city and divesting the urban core of the financial and personal investment of its former residents. In the years that Prince George's County has been growing with the middle-class Black residents leaving the district, the wealth in PG County has been steadily increasing, while at the same time the wealth in the Northeast and Southeast Quadrants has been decreasing.[32]

One way to measure this change in wealth is by looking at the DC wards. The District of Columbia is divided up into eight wards, each of which is further divided into advisory neighborhood commissions (ANC). The wards, a further subdivision of each quadrant, are used for neighborhood governance and to elect equitable representation to the citywide government. The District is separated into eight wards: Wards 1, 2, 3, and 4 are in the Northwest Quadrant; Ward 5 is the majority of the Northeast Quadrant; Ward 6 encompasses the smallest quadrant, the Southwest Quadrant, plus the Southeast Quadrant west of the Anacostia River; and Wards 7 and 8 make up the remainder of the Southeast Quadrant. From 1980 to 2011 the poverty rate in Ward 8, which includes Historic Anacostia, rose from 27 percent to 36 percent, in comparison to the DC average of 19 percent and 18 percent, respectively. In fact, from 1980 to 2011 Ward 8 had the highest rate among DC's eight wards for both poverty and unemployment.[33]

PG County, meanwhile, shows clearly the effects of the exodus of Washington, DC's affluent Black residents. In 2011, of the neighborhoods in the county where the average household income surpassed $100,000 per year, three-quarters were majority Black, and PG County has come to be known for having one of the highest concentrations of Black wealth in the United States.[34] By 2015

FIGURE 1. Map of the District of Columbia and Surrounding Counties.
(© 2021 Newbcreations. Used with permission.)

PG County was over 60 percent African American, with a Black population just over 560,000. In the process of this exodus, however, the same racial divides that were once evident in the District have become mirrored in PG County. The *Washington Post* reported in 2011 that over 27 percent of PG County neighborhoods had 85 percent or more same-ethnicity residents—meaning the racial divides that characterized Washington, DC, have continued as the populations have moved into PG County.

The flight of middle-income Black residents to PG County in the 1970s left behind the lower-income Black residents in the Northeast and Southeast Quadrants. For every eastern ward except Ward 6, the percentage of residents living in poverty has increased with each decennial census.[35] This creates a stark divide across the District of Columbia/Maryland border, as the wealthy Black residents who've left enjoy lower poverty and unemployment rates in the county immediately adjacent to the one they left behind.

The region which resulted from this migration was one in which African American populations were at the same time emboldened and disenfranchised: middle-class people in PG County experienced a surge in economic opportunity that was protected by the continued strong job opportunities in the District along with the proceeds from their home sales in DC, while the African American communities which remained in the District struggled after having been divested of their resources due to the riots. In the 1970s, as Mr. Moore discusses, DC was a place where an incoming African American man might expect the streets to be "paved with gold." But the exodus of the middle-class Black community means that DC is now home to an African American community that no longer is by law separated by race but instead within itself is increasingly segregated by class, and whose members must engage in practices of identity formation and maintenance in order to fit in within the DC that *is* instead of the DC that *was*. The chief places for these sites of identity formation and negotiation are the places where Black Washingtonians have always made their homes: places like Historic Anacostia.

### The Making of a Black Place: The History of Anacostia

The land that is now the neighborhood of Anacostia once belonged to the Nacotchtank Indians, from whom the name Anacostia derives.[36] Explorer Capt. John Smith drew a map published in 1612 that mapped the "V" of the Potomac River and the Eastern Branch River (later the Anacostia). By the late 1660s white settlers had overtaken the land on the banks of the Eastern Branch, driving out the Nacotchtank Tribe. Throughout the 1700s white settlement increased in the area. The region south and east of the Eastern Branch River was annexed in order to provide military defense when the new federal city was officially established in 1800. In that same year James Barry, a farmer and friend of George Washington, bought a large tract of land on the hills overlooking the Eastern Branch, on which he built a plantation. The Washington Navy Yard was established across the river.[37]

In the early 1800s, as the United States slowly rolled toward civil war, increasing racial tensions in the country were reflected in the growth of Anacostia. To the east of Barry's plantation, a community of freed slaves called Good Hope was founded.[38] Throughout the 1800s Anacostia grew as a settlement for successful free Black people, with several former slaves becoming DC's first African American lawyers and ministers and establishing the city's first African American churches and schools. In 1854 the Union Land Association, founded by developers John Van Hook, John Fox, and John Dobler, created Uniontown (now downtown Historic Anacostia) to provide housing for the white workers employed at the Navy Yard. Because the Navy Yard bridge (now called the Eleventh Street bridge[39]) connects with the heart of Uniontown, this area at the end of the bridge became predominately white. Van Hook at the time owned an estate he named Cedar Hill, situated at the top of what is now Fourteenth and W Street SE.[40]

In 1862 the Emancipation Act freed slaves in the District of Columbia, and not long after the slaves in other states in the Confederacy.[41] This necessitated a large-scale operation to assist the number of freed slaves, including with their relocation. The Bureau of Refugees, Freedmen, and Abandoned Lands, better known as the Freedmen's Bureau, was established in 1865; among the operations which the Freedmen's Bureau oversaw was the division of the James Barry property into parcels which the newly freed slaves could purchase. Many of these families went on to slowly build homes on their lands, doing construction at night after long days working across the river in Washington City. In 1875 the Anacostia and Potomac River Street Railroad Company was organized under "Boss" Alexander Shephardson, bringing streetcars across the river to Anacostia.[42] In 1890 the Pennsylvania Avenue Bridge was built, linking Southeast DC north of the Anacostia River to locations further east, and providing another important link into Maryland. In 1877 abolitionist Frederick Douglass and his wife, Anna, purchased Cedar Hill, becoming residents of Uniontown. Douglass went on to become known as "the Sage of Anacostia"; he was nominated to the new city council when the cities of Washington, Georgetown, and Washington County were merged to officially become the District of Columbia, and he became chair of the Freedmen's Bureau.[43]

The early 1900s saw increased investment from the city into the neighborhood, while the surroundings remained rural. Many older residents interviewed for this book recall having outhouses, outdoor washtubs, and water pumps as late as the 1940s.[44] Importantly, during this time the neighborhood retained the racial makeup that the post–Civil War settlement patterns had established: the community of former slaves and their descendants, including a thriving Black middle class, continued to live in the western part of the area, in the Hillsdale community that later became Barry Farm.[45] Meanwhile, Uniontown remained white.[46] Even with this segregation, residents often recall the first half of the twentieth century as being unusually harmonious for a southern city. While the Jim Crow laws that governed relationships between Black and white Americans throughout the south were not officially enforced in Washington, DC, their existence in the neighboring southern state of Virginia meant they were de facto codified into the expectations of white Washingtonians.

After the 1968 riots, many of the white residents of Uniontown fled to the suburbs, replaced at first by Black residents from nearby Hillsdale. But over the decades those longtime Black residents also trickled out to the suburbs in a second wave of flight.

With the reduction in the population's socioeconomic resources, the neighborhood began to decline: a noticeable number of homes and buildings in the area were abandoned and left so for decades, while violent crime became abundant.[47] For the last four decades Anacostia has seen increasing poverty and unemployment levels that have solidified the neighborhood's international reputation as a place one simply is not to go. In 2013 a *Washington Post* blog included Anacostia in a list of "16 American Cities Foreign Governments Warn Their Citizens About," quoting the French Foreign Ministry as recommending their nationals not go to Anacostia, day or night.[48]

That their neighborhood has a reputation for being undesirable is a fact with which all of the interviewees for this book contend every time they talk about it.[49] This negative reputation has led white Washingtonians to be generally reluctant to visit, or particularly to live in Anacostia, which has historically ensured that Anacostia remained a neighborhood with a strong African American identity, reaching a peak in 2015 of 95 percent of residents claiming the identity "Black alone" in the census. As home prices have risen throughout the remainder of Washington, DC, however, residents who a decade ago might have sought homes in the Northwest Quadrant's Mount Pleasant neighborhood are now buying homes in Anacostia; in 2011 a three-bedroom home that might have run upward of $750,000 in other parts of the city could be found in Anacostia for around $250,000.[50] However, perhaps in part because of Anacostia's history and its perceived reputation, the first wave of new residents of the neighborhood were middle- and upper-class Blacks who began moving in during the late 2000s and early 2010s. Some had grown up in Anacostia and returned after living elsewhere, and others had never lived in Anacostia before. Though a few non-Black newcomers began to arrive in the late 2010s, the first wave of change, with its racial homogeneity, is the focus of this work.[51] This relatively racially homogenous shift in socioeconomic demographics, an unusual pattern for a gentrifying locale, makes Anacostia a perfect site for exploring the ways that residents' language use exemplifies and creates connections between racial identity and a sense of place.

## Black Spaces, Black Reality

When Mr. Moore came to Washington, he expected to find a city which had all but rolled out a red carpet out for him. He expected a thriving "intelligentsia," ample opportunity, and for his fellow Black residents to welcome him with open arms. Instead, however, the city let him down. "I thought [Washington, DC] was extremely dirty and nasty," he says. "When I first came to Washington to see that, and see all the– the devastation after the riots, and everything, I was extremely disappointed."

But then he crossed a river.

> Southeast didn't look anything like what was in Northwest. It– I said to myself it was almost like I wasn't even in in in Washington, DC. I don't know if that is because Southeast didn't have the businesses that—and the business corridors as U Street and and Fourteen Street and and Connecticut and downtown had. I just don't know. Because I wasn't here. I didn't grow up here. But all I do know is, when I came across the bridge, and saw some of these homes over here it was more like what I was accustomed to in North Carolina. So I was very, very appreciative that if I wanted a garden in my yard, I knew I could have a garden in my yard and I'd have to only contend with the rodents and those kind of animals that would eat my food like rabbits.

Mr. Moore's juxtaposition of the "dirty and nasty" Northwest against the bucolic Anacostia part of Southeast inverts the general narrative about places west and east of the river. Anacostia's reputation within the greater Washington area is one of crime, poverty, and general undesirability.[52] Taxicabs are known to refuse to drop off or pick up patrons there, a problem that has only intensified because the gig economy allows Uber and Lyft drivers, who can even more thoroughly follow their own desires, to simply avoid taking fares that originate or terminate in the area.[53] Northwest, locals say, is desirable and clean; Southeast is where you don't go.

Yet this is not at all how Mr. Moore experiences the neighborhood. When he talks about Anacostia and its surrounds, it is the Northwest Quadrant that is "dirty and nasty" and Southeast is a bucolic locale that feels like his native North Carolina. This contrast across the city, and the comparison to his original home, serves to change the way that his audience is meant to interpret Southeast and flip the script on the relationship between Southeast and Northwest. This contrast does not happen through a physical change—it is not that Mr. Moore is part of some beautification committee or involved in some kind of neighborhood revival. No, the way he *talks* about the neighborhood reimagines the neighborhood from a different perspective—one which I will argue is fundamentally rooted in the Black culture and experience of Anacostia.

Sociological, anthropological, and geographical approaches which center Black experience reveal that the ways Black people experience urban spaces are not the same as those of white residents in the same space. Studies in major metropolitan areas have shown that while white investors might frame urban change as the creation of commodity, Black residents often understand it as the taking of space.[54] In the face of racialized denial of claims to space, middle-class Blacks find themselves as brokers, mediating between the powerful urban planners and developers who wish to stake claims on space while grounding their conversations in their lived experience as Black Americans.

When we reconceive place from the desires and needs of Black inhabitants, we see it differently. We see the entire United States as "the South," as Malcolm X claimed; we see places where Black people are treated differentially but also differently; and we see that there is no magical "North" that is devoid of discrimination or where Black experience is unremarkable. We see the pockets of Black experience and the ways they make safe spaces for Black people and create Black communities where whites and outsiders are likely to see only problems.

DC is a particularly important place to understand when considering the role of Black lived experience in the face of urban change. It is what Isabel Wilkerson calls the "honorary north": officially south of the Mason-Dixon Line but promoted to the status of an imagined, antidiscriminatory North by virtue of its being the capital of the Union.[55] Its long history of African American achievement, leading to the unparalleled concentration of African American wealth in the region, makes it an important place to use for understanding the ways that race, class, and belonging intersect.

Centering Black lived experience when we look at the ways that people make claims on their space reveals the ways in which race both proxies for and mediates other identities of class and location. Race can proxy in a negative way, as when arguments about property values and public housing serve to ghettoize African American communities by veiling racist arguments as arguments about the free market.[56] But race can also proxy in the other direction, as when a Black community serves as a reason to reject negative characterization of a space. For someone like Mr. Moore, that lived experience is reflected in his language: the ways that Northwest becomes "dirty and nasty" and Southeast becomes the place where the biggest bother one might encounter are a few opportunistic rabbits in your garden. In the language of Black experience, a crime-ridden location becomes a safe one; a dirty one becomes a beautiful one (reframings that are explored in greater depth in chapters 1 and 2).

The changes taking place in Washington, DC, are not unlike changes that are taking place elsewhere across the United States, places like Harlem and Southside Chicago.[57] These changes occur rapidly as the demographics of cities recreate and redefine who is an urban dweller, changing from poor and working class people of color to highly educated, wealthy whites.[58] Who is from the city is changing. Yet as city governments continue to attempt to not displace existing residents as urban centers make way for newcomers, understanding the claims those residents make on their space has never been more important.[59] Using language as a lens for understanding the ways that Black space is claimed and preserved can yield strategies to help preserve Black existence in an increasingly changing cityscape.

### Communities of Practice and the Practices of Place

Mr. Moore's hopefulness about the city of Washington, DC, demonstrates the power that Washington and other Chocolate Cities have in the Black imagination. The ways in which they have historically drawn and encouraged Black culture and Black community distinctly define Chocolate Cities. Chocolate Cities are about place-making—the ways in which a physical space becomes imbued with social meaning, as linguists Ron and Suzy Wong Scollon put it.[60] Anacostia is one such place for Black social meaning: it is a physical space which, due to its history, has been instantiated as a place of Black culture and history, situated within the Chocolate City of Washington, DC. Studying how Black residents make sense of the neighborhood through their discourse, through their framings and reframings, and through the linguistic system itself—which together I am terming the *linguistic practices of place*—shows how Black people make specifically Black space: how it is imbued with racial identity to create the sense of opportunity and hope that has historically drawn people there.

That language is connected to both place identity and race identity has a long history in the field of sociolinguistics, and it is useful to understand that history in order to explain how the situation in Anacostia complicates our understanding of these connections.

Many of the earliest studies that could be considered sociolinguistic studies (though the subfield would not be defined until much later) are studies of the relationships between language and space. Dialectological surveys were principally concerned with establishing the patterns by which speakers differed according to their senses of place; for example, exactly where the line in the physical landscape was where a *dragonfly* became a *darning needle*.[61]

As sociolinguistics moved forward as a discipline, linguists began to explore the ways in which language differed systematically, and not only by the spatial organization of speakers but also by the ways those speakers were grouped socially. These *speech communities* were sometimes locations where those speakers lived, but other times the speakers' social class, gender identity, and, importantly, ethnicity could also create communities.[62] These studies made the important contribution of showing predictable patterns in language use based on speakers' intersecting membership in certain social groups, and they paved the way for increased linguistic understanding of the patterning of nonstandardized English varieties.[63]

One danger of grouping people based on external definitions of their identities is the over-assumption of homogeneity within those groups: it is not the case that every working-class African American person speaks the same way. That said, the speech community approach to sociolinguistic studies had several benefits: it documented the systematicity of stigmatized varieties and it showed that the study of these varieties made important contributions to our understanding of linguistic structure more generally.[64] In addition, it acknowledged to some extent the lack of homogeneity between subsets of speech communities or intersections of different kinds of identity.

An issue of particular importance to the variety explored in this volume—African American Language—has been its seeming aregionality. Given the history of sociolinguistics and its embeddedness in the dialectological surveys of the 1940s, the appeal of a variety whose features seem *not* to be about where speakers are from but rather where they are tied to a different social identity—ethnicity—is too tempting to resist.[65] As a result, regional differences in aspects of African American Language (AAL) were often omitted or underplayed in early explorations of the variety.[66]

But the specific relationships between language and place and language and race are more complicated than this, and more recent scholarship has connected African American Language use with both racial and regional identity. African American speakers in Tennessee sound different from those in Iowa, possibly because of different rates of exposure to Northern, white varieties of English.[67] African Americans and people belonging to other ethnic groups often do not participate in the sound changes taking place within the white communities around them.[68] African Americans in Texas are notable users of a variety that is at once characteristic of rural speech more generally, of Texan speech specifically, and of some features more commonly found in other African American Language–speaking communities in the United States.[69] And other linguists who have worked specifically on Historic Anacostia have found that some speakers here do not always pronounce vowels the same way even as other African American speakers elsewhere in DC do.[70]

In each case, the experience of being an African American in a locale will be different than being a white person in the same locale, and it will also be different than the experience of being an African American in a different locale. African American Language, then, becomes not an aregional monolith but rather a variable way of mediating the intersection between race and place. A place like Washington, DC, especially a smaller neighborhood within that city which have been understood as Black places for many decades, provides both a physical and an intellectual site for understanding how these experiences of being African American and speaking African American Language come to mean particular things about being part of the Black community.

The ways in which language not only mediates one's membership in a given group but also serves as a means for speakers to display their relationships to that group calls for a more nuanced understanding of what constitutes a community in the first place. Unlike a speech community approach, which generally defines a community from the outside and then looks for ways that the members of that community use language to demonstrate their ties to the community and to one another, the *community of practice* approach defines the community from the inside, centering on how the members of the community use language to demonstrate their ties to one another.

The communities of practice framework stems from work by educational theorists Jean Lave and Etienne Wenger in the 1990s.[71] Lave and Wenger propose that a community of practice is made up of three necessary components: the domain, or the locus around which the community is based; the people who make up the community; and the practice or the endeavor around which the community is organized. They argue that as learners become involved in authentic experiences embedded within an appropriate cultural context, their participation in the community of practice with other learners ultimately enables their growth from novice to expert in whatever endeavor in which the group is engaged.

Linguistics is one of multiple allied fields in which researchers have adopted the community of practice theory.[72] The theory allows linguists to explain hyperlocal language practices—which are exactly the opposite of the fetishized, supralocal language practices that drove many of the early studies of African Americans' language. Instead of beginning with a group of people who share some sort of externally definable boundary—living in the same place, belonging to the same racial or ethnic group, being of the same age cohort—community of practice studies in linguistics begin with the speakers themselves and attempt to classify the ways in which their language practices tie them to one another.

Thanks to community of practice theory, the field of sociolinguistics has, in recent years, made significant strides in considering how individuals shape their own language use and the ways that individual patterns show what is happening on a broader scale. Thus, instead of the top-down approach so common fifty years ago, the approach now is decisively bottom-up: taking the speakers as the primary source of information about what a given change in language means instead of inferring from patterns that differentiate externally defined groups. While sociolinguists may no longer see these large categories and these regional boundaries as the dividing lines that give us the most important information about what different speakers' language use means, the people we study want to know whether or not people "talk differently" based on these same large-scale categories of place and race. When speakers hear *community*, they understand it not within the community of practice paradigm but in terms of the neighborhood, the people, and the history of Historic Anacostia. This nonspecialist definition of *community*, therefore, will always be primary, and it is here that any study of a community's language ought to begin.

In this book I explore the ways by which language becomes a means of reinforcing the community that speakers inhabit. It is not solely about African American identity, though African American identity is part of being from an African American neighborhood in a Chocolate City. It is not solely about place identity, though being from Anacostia is part of the identity that creates Anacostia. Instead of looking at speakers as being part of a community of practice or a speech community based on place, I ask instead how the residents of Historic Anacostia participate in the practice of place: how they *do* the identity of being from Historic Anacostia and the specific role that language practices play in reinforcing that identity.

As I explore this practice of place, I ask how Anacostians enact their sense of place linguistically. How does their practice of place interact and intersect with their practice of race? What can this practice of place tell us about what it means to be an African American at a time when countless US cities, including Chocolate Cities, are changing?

I root these questions in Chocolate Cities Sociology, Black Geography, and Black Linguistics. Each of these approaches holds one similar tenet: Black experience changes the nature of lived experience substantially enough from the experience of whites that any study of these experiences must originate from and center on the Black people who experience them. As I ask what "Historic Anacostia" means, I pull answers only from those for whom Historic Anacostia means home.

The interviews for this book took place in two time periods and captured two different phases of the changes taking place in Anacostia. In 2011 the demographic makeup of Anacostia was beginning to change, a fact the *Washington Post* captured as it reported on the influx of Black middle-class Washingtonians to the neighborhood. A fellow student and I together conducted eighteen interviews of African American longtime community members from 2011 to 2013 as part of our doctoral work in sociolinguistics, with interviewees from a range of ages and socioeconomic statuses. I returned in 2015–17 to conduct interviews with an additional sixteen African American longtime residents of Anacostia as well as one newcomer couple. By this time the Eleventh Street bridge reconstruction was complete, making it more convenient for people from the Northwest and Northeast Quadrants to come into Anacostia. New apartments were already springing up on Martin Luther King Avenue.

The bulk of my analysis derives from these thirty-four interviews, which also provide the data for my quantitative analysis of morphosyntactic features (see chapter 3). I am concerned principally with the ways in which a historically Black neighborhood identity manifests through language practice. Also, the racial distribution of interviews is not unrepresentative of the neighborhood as a whole; during the time period in which these interviews were conducted, census surveys recorded Anacostia as over 95 percent "Black alone." There have always been white residents in Anacostia as well as white Washingtonians who, while living elsewhere, worked and experienced life and investment in Anacostia. I have omitted them from this work not to obscure the fact that they exist but rather to focus the analysis on the group most directly involved in this book's key questions about the intersections of race, place, and language.

## Naming Race and Language

A brief note on terminology and technique is warranted here. Throughout this work I often follow the practice of using *Black* to refer to people of the African diaspora. In particular I use and capitalize *Black* to emphasize the shared culture that has developed in the United States as the result of discrimination, racism, and the lasting sociocultural effects of the institution of slavery. Like others who center race and racism, I lowercase white because this same cohesion does not always exist among European Americans; here *Black* is placed equal in footing to capitalized European ethnicities like Irish or Polish, which represent identities of the specific traceable homeland that most African Americans are denied because of the brutal history of the transatlantic slave trade. This book argues that the culture created by the reading of race in this country explains why a neighborhood like Anacostia develops in the first place—divisions of space ultimately correspond to divisions of race. When I am referring to racial designation as an adjective, I use *African American*. It should be noted that the interviewees use *Black* and *African American* interchangeably and in ways that their interviewer may affect. I leave the terms the interviewees use exactly as they use them.

A second important note is the choice to term the language variety discussed in this book as African American Language. English, within the Black American context, is somewhat fraught within the sociocultural context of the African descendants of slaves; its supposed neutrality masks particular colonial practices and erasure of certain kinds of language practices that are not associated with English but rather with other languages that enslaved peoples brought with them. Over the decades, as the terms used to describe the population of peoples who descend from enslaved African people in the United States have changed, so too have the terms for the systematically distinct language varieties they use: it has been "Nonstandard Negro English," "Negro Dialect," "Ebonics," "Black English Vernacular," "Black English," "African American Vernacular English" (often abbreviated AAVE), and "African American English," with AAVE and Ebonics being the two most commonly recognized terms among nonspecialists.[73] Still other scholars make a choice of term in order to reflect the political situation of the language and its speakers: for instance, April Baker-Bell chooses "Black Language" to both acknowledge that "Black speech is the continuation in the African in an American Context" and to align with Black Liberation movements such as Black Lives Matter.[74] I am engaging with the entire idea of culturally Black ways of speaking and the ways in which that way of speaking has implications for imbuing a place with Black culture. Thus I choose to use what Sonja Lanehart refers to as the "less marked" version, African American Language, in order to encompass the widest breadth of possible meanings that this encompasses: a variety which involves systematic differences from white American varieties at every level of the linguistic system that is not "slang," not "broken," not "deficient," and, importantly, is uniquely Black.[75]

In the same vein, throughout this work I aim to present data in an accessible and readable way while still retaining the precise language moves made by interviewees. I mean to retain the poetic rhythm of African American Language, which has its roots in freedom songs and Black preaching. At the same time, and mindful of the ways Black Language is consistently denigrated and seen as inferior to white varieties, I wish not to accidentally give the impression that the interviewees in this book are somehow less well-spoken by retaining speech disfluencies which characterize all human speech in places where they are usually edited out in professional writing. To balance these competing aims, within block quotations I have edited out most repetitions and speech disfluencies except where they contribute to the poetic rhythm of the interviewee's style. Where I analyze word-by-word, I present my interviewees' speech in unedited form, broken into numbered intonation units, as is more typical for analysis of morphosyntactic features. I also follow the customary approach to italicize a word (rather than use scare quotes) when the word is being referred to as a word.

Finally, while the final product of this book is the result of careful work with several editors, I also wish to preserve at least some of the nuance of my own grammatical idiosyncrasies. Language simply *is*, and while we may futilely attempt to control it with grammar guides and textbooks and admonitions, it continues to change over time as speakers use it. I choose in many instances in this book to disregard prescriptive adherence to the more conservative forms of many language changes in progress. I split infinitives; I use *data* and *they* in the singular; I use words which are in the process of shifting meaning with their newer definitions; and, as in the previous sentence, I often pay no heed to the restriction status of relative clauses and use the relative pronoun that sounds best to my ear. My goal in leaving these in is to emphasize that "good" language encompasses all language, especially Black language, and to preserve for corpus linguists of the future a clear example of what a highly educated Black woman's writing looks like in the early twenty-first century.

## Outline of the Book

Each chapter of this book explores the forms taken by the linguistic practice of place, focusing on how groups of practices relate to one another. Chapter 1 explores the ways in which Big-D Discourses erase the existence of African American gentrifiers and in turn iconize the processes of gentrification as being about race rather than about class.[76] I show further that even as demographics indicate that the people moving into Historic Anacostia are predominately Black, neighborhood residents still talk about the process as being driven almost exclusively by whites. Deictic markers allow residents to juxtapose an "us," the DC Black, to a white "them," which reinforces cohesion among the Black community. Ultimately these practices work in tandem to reinforce the communal understanding of gentrification as being principally an issue of race.

In chapter 2 I argue that the aspects of the community which residents choose to talk about serve to reject the outsider characterization of their community as impoverished, dirty, and crime-ridden. Using the concepts of forced-positioning and framing, I show how residents carefully emphasize the community's beauty, the safety the community's cohesion creates, and its desirability, in order to reframe the deficit perspective from which outsiders approach Anacostia and reposition it as a place where any person would want to be.[77]

Chapter 3 argues that the identities of place become commingled with identities of race not only in larger discourses but also at the level of individuals' morphosyntax. I trace how features of AAL pattern differently across the different topics that interviewees discuss, and I determine that topics related to place identities do pattern in a remarkably similar way to topics related to race identity—suggesting that these identities are closely linked. This linkage allows AAL to serve as a resource for expressing place identity for middle-class African American residents of Anacostia who, based on their socioeconomic demographics, might otherwise be categorized with the gentrifying outsiders. It allows them to appeal to a racial identity that implicitly criticizes change.

Chapter 4 explains how Black community language translates into Black community power. I demonstrate that DC's physical geography is mapped onto race in a way that characterizes Southeast DC as being Black space, and I show how the kinds of practices of place I explore serve, in turn, to stake claims on that Black space, to highlight Black success within that space, and to claim agency for those who live there. While the link between African American identity and place and class identity is often exploited to negative ends, such as when city planners talk about "blight" and "property values" as a means for not directly talking about a place as being African American, I draw on the findings in the previous chapters and suggest that the reverse can also be true: language that links Black success to a physical locale points to a way African American residents can lay claim to a physical space. When the community identity is a positive identity, so too is Black identity; this shift empowers Blacks more broadly.

In the conclusion I consider the ways that these intersections of race and place identity have broader implications for our understanding of how African Americans relate to place, as urban centers continue to change in the twenty-first century. Synthesizing the linguistic practices of place, I show how connecting Black identity to place in the positive ways that Anacostians do in their discourse has important implications for understanding race and place more generally. When Blackness is valued, and when Black presence in a place makes it valued, the kinds of "solutions" to urban problems often sought by white outsiders are revealed as unwanted and untenable. In turn, solutions that serve and empower Black community must be sought. I further demonstrate the importance of studying Black language and Black discourse in situ, that is, not only as a construct unto itself but also in the ways in which it is deployed in the maintenance of place identity. Finally, I point to how these Black linguistic practices are intertwined with class identity as well as place, and I argue for the need for more intersectional approaches to sociolinguistic study. While other studies show that African American communities often buy into and reinforce these socioeconomic narratives about gentrification, my work shows that these understandings are nevertheless understood as racial and it points toward a way that we can understand and empower people through these connections of race and locality.[78]

This work considers what it means to be not merely *from* a place but to be a specific person from *that* place. When Black people use language to reinforce ideologically Black places, it changes our understanding of what it means when those Black places become encroached upon. This book explores those changed understandings and who defines the lines between Blacks and whites, between poverty and prosperity. Ultimately it explains what it means for all Black people when one community crosses the river.

## Notes

1. Rampersad, *Life of Langston Hughes*.
2. National Underground Railroad Freedom Center, "About Us."
3. US Congress, "Act for Establishing."
4. Jaffe, *Dream City*.
5. Casselman, "Virginia Portion"; Hutchinson, *Anacostia Story*.
6. Casselman, "Virginia Portion."
7. US Congress, "Act for Establishing" (emphasis added).
8. Gutheim and Lee, *Worthy of the Nation*; Casselman, "Virginia Portion."
9. Anacostia Waterfront Trust, "Anacostia in History."
10. Throughout this book I refer to the community members I interviewed using pseudonyms. Out of sensitivity to the long history of whites calling African Americans by their first name to indicate a lack of respect, I have chosen to use first name pseudonyms for community members who welcomed me to use their first names. For those interviewees whom I, a young woman researcher, address by title and surname, I use a title and pseudonym surname in this book.
11. Many Black Washingtonians, especially those who have lived in Washington for several generations, trace their roots as descendants of slaves in North Carolina. North Carolina was many times invoked by my interviewees when they were asked about their metalinguistic awareness of differences in speech varieties (see chap. 3). North Carolina is almost universally framed as "the South" in comparison to DC. Wilkerson, *Warmth of Other Suns*; Gregory, *Southern Diaspora*.
12. George Clinton, Bootsy Collins, and Bernie Worrell, "Chocolate City" (*Chocolate City*, Casablanca Records, 1975).

13. Smithsonian Anacostia Museum, *Black Washingtonians*.

14. Smithsonian Anacostia Museum, *Black Washingtonians*.

15. Wilkerson, *Warmth of Other Suns*; Trotter and Painter, *Great Migration*.

16. Hunter and Robinson, *Chocolate Cities*.

17. Hunter and Robinson, 2.

18. Prince (African Americans and Gentrification) documents over a dozen locales in DC with historical ties to slave trading.

19. Unless stated otherwise, all demographic and population data about Washington, DC, are taken from the relevant years' US Census Bureau data tables, accessed through www.census.gov.

20. Graham, *Our Kind of People*; Gale, *Washington, D.C.*

21. *Washington Post*, "The Four Days in 1968 That Reshaped D.C.," *Washington Post*, June 15, 2018; Smithsonian Anacostia Museum, *Black Washingtonians*; Jaffe, *Dream City*.

22. *Washington Post*, "Four Days in 1968"; Smithsonian Anacostia Museum, *Black Washingtonians*; Jaffe, *Dream City*.

23. *Washington Post*, "Four Days in 1968"; Smithsonian Anacostia Museum, *Black Washingtonians*; Jaffe, *Dream City*.

24. *Washington Post*, "Four Days in 1968"; Smithsonian Anacostia Museum, *Black Washingtonians*; Jaffe, *Dream City*.

25. While the community's name is officially "Barry Farm," it is most often colloquially referred to as "Barry Farms." When I quote an interviewee I use the term used by the interviewee.

26. Gale, *Washington, D.C.*

27. Ann Mariano, "Survey of Area Apartments Finds Rental Bias Common: Whites Said to Be Favored in 54% of Tests," *Washington Post*, September 30, 1986.

28. Gale, *Washington, D.C.*; Prince, *African Americans and Gentrification*.

29. National Park Service, "The L'Enfant and McMillan Plans."

30. Bernstein Management Corp., "1600 Pennsylvania Avenue."

31. As in much of the United States, this pattern is due in part to racially restrictive housing covenants, which kept African Americans from owning homes in the Northwest Quadrant but was also influenced by the development of corridors of African American residents in parts of the city, such as in the Shaw neighborhood, which surrounds Howard University. See e.g., Prince, *African Americans and Gentrification*.

32. Emily Wax, "'Gentrification' Covers Black and White Middle-Class Home Buyers in the District," *Washington Post*, July 29, 2011; Prince, *African Americans and Gentrification*.

33. There is some anecdotal evidence that African American DC residents are likely to refer to the ward system when talking about their sense of place. Differences between Ward 7 and Ward 8 were brought up frequently in the interviews I conducted, residents were very likely to identify themselves and others as being a part of Ward 8, and residents identified their concerns as being related to the ward rather than to the neighborhood.

34. Morello and Melnick, "District Grows Younger and More White, Census Statistics Show," *Washington Post*, June 12, 2013; Wiggins, Morello, and Keating, "Prince George's County: Growing, and Growing More Segregated, Census Shows," *Washington Post*, October 30, 2011.

35. Ward 6 contains the neighborhood of Capitol Hill, one of the only eastern neighborhoods which has a large white population in the 2000 map in figure 1. By 2010 that area had an even smaller density of African American residents. It is likely that the reduction in poverty in this ward between 2000 and 2007–11 can be attributed to middle-income whites moving into that neighborhood, one of the few in the Southeast and Northeast Quadrants that at present are considered to be gentrifying.

36. Hutchinson, *Anacostia Story*; Smithsonian Anacostia Museum, *Black Washingtonians*.

37. Hutchinson, *Anacostia Story*; Jaffe, *Dream City*; Smithsonian Anacostia Museum, *Black Washingtonians*.

38. Dale, *Village That Shaped Us*; Smithsonian Anacostia Museum, *Black Washingtonians*.

39. Hutchinson, *Anacostia Story*; Smithsonian Anacostia Museum, *Black Washingtonians*; Muller, *Frederick Douglass in Washington, D.C.*

40. Muller, *Frederick Douglass in Washington, D.C.*; Fitzpatrick and Goodwin, *Guide to Black Washington*.

41. Fitzpatrick and Goodwin, *Guide to Black Washington*.

42. Fitzpatrick and Goodwin, *Guide to Black Washington*; Smithsonian Anacostia Museum, *Black Washingtonians*; Hutchinson, *Anacostia Story*.

43. Jaffe, *Dream City*; Muller, *Frederick Douglass in Washington, D.C.*; Hutchinson, *Anacostia Story*.

44. For example, see the quote from Carol in chap. 2.

45. Dale, *Village That Shaped Us*; Hutchinson, *Anacostia Story*.

46. Hutchinson, *Anacostia Story*; Jaffe, *Dream City*.

47. Robinson, *Disintegration*; Wax, "Gentrification."

48. Reid Wilson, "16 American Cities Foreign Governments Warn Their Citizens About," *Washington Post*, November 14, 2013.

49. See also Lee, "Discourse on Southeast's Bad Reputation."

50. See Modan, *Turf Wars*, for an explanation of what was going on in Mount Pleasant in the early twenty-first century. For 2011 statistics, see Wax, "Gentrification."

51. Estimates from the 2017 census, the most recent as of this writing, show white residents comprise less than 3 percent of the neighborhood population.

52. See Lee, "Discourse on Southeast's Bad Reputation," for a discussion of this outsider positioning of the neighborhood.

53. Benjamin Freed, "Lyft Suspends Driver Accused of Not Picking Up Customers from Southeast DC," *Washingtonian*, March 21, 2016. In 2016 a Lyft driver was suspended after being accused of racial discrimination by the DC Office of Human Rights. In 2013 a study by a local news agency found that over 30 percent of DC cab drivers ignored Black potential customers, often using location as a proxy.

54. Prince, *African Americans and Gentrification*; Woldoff, *White Flight/Black Flight*.

55. Wilkerson, *Warmth of Other Suns*.

56. Pattillo, "Black on the Block"; N. Smith, *New Urban Frontier*.

57. Prince, *Constructing Belonging*; Pattillo, "Black on the Block" and *Black Picket Fences*.

58. Alpert, "DC Has Almost No White Residents." Only 2 percent of the 2016 electorate in Greater Washington consisted of whites without college degrees.

59. In 2015, in light of the declining African American population in the city, Mayor Muriel Bowser authorized the creation of an African American Affairs office. This office was seen by many as an acknowledgment of the drastic demographic shift the city had already experienced: from 1970 to 2015 all DC affairs had been "African American affairs."

60. Scollon and Scollon, *Discourses in Place*.

61. Kurath and McDavid, *Pronunciation of English*. The line in the sand for that change is approximately north of the Ohio River, though modern dialectology surveys of the United States generally find that "darning needle" is obsolete. See *Dictionary of American Regional English*.

62. Hymes, "Speech Community"; Morgan, "African American Speech Community." Hymes and Morgan, in their chapters in the same volume, provide thorough explanations of the concept of the speech community and how the theory can be practicably applied to African American speech communities.

63. See Labov, *Language in the Inner City*; Wolfram, *Sociolinguistic*

*Description*; Shuy, Wolfram, and Riley, *Field Techniques*; and Fasold, *Tense Marking in Black English*, for examples of these early studies.

64. Bucholtz, "Sociolinguistic Nostalgia." Bucholtz claims that the complexity of African American Language was simplified to focus on its most highly vernacular features in order to strategically emphasize its patterning to those who might consider it pathological. Rickford, "Unequal Partnership"; Wolfram, "Sociolinguistic Myths" and "Sociolinguistic Construction."

65. See Kurath and McDavid, *Pronunciation of English*.

66. See Wolfram, "Sociolinguistic Myths" and "Sociolinguistic Construction."

67. Hinton and Pollock, "Regional Variations."

68. Hoffman and Walker, "Ethnolects and the City."

69. Cukor-Avila, "Co-Existing Grammars"; Bailey and Cukor-Avila, "Rural Texas."

70. Lee, "Phonetic Variation."

71. Lave and Wenger, *Situated Learning*.

72. Eckert and McConnell-Ginet, "Communities of Practice"; Bucholtz, "Why Be Normal?" Eckert and McConnell-Ginet make a compelling case for the use of a community of practice approach in sociolinguistics, and Bucholtz explicitly builds on this call by showing how the approach is more useful than traditional approaches favored by variationist linguistics in explaining the language use of a self-defined group of high school girls.

73. Charting the entire scope of these changes is not necessary for the arguments of this volume. However, those interested in a nuanced discussion of the development of these terms and the way they have captured changing ideas about African Americans and the language variety many of them speak would do well to consult Smitherman, "What Is Africa to Me?"; Baugh, "Politicization of Changing Terms"; and Wolfram's chapter in *The Oxford Handbook of African American Language*, "Sociolinguistic Construction."

74. Baker-Bell, *Linguistic Justice*, 3.

75. Lanehart, *Oxford Handbook*, 3.

76. Chafe, *Discourse, Consciousness, and Time*.

77. Harré and Van Langenhove, *Positioning Theory*; Harré and Moghaddam, *Self and Others*; Goffman, *Frame Analysis*; Goffman, "Presentation of Self"; Tannen, "What's in a Frame?"

78. Pattillo, *Black on the Block*.

# "I've Never Known a White Person to Live on Hill Street"

Racializing Gentrification through Discourse

## Introduction: The Metonymic Neighborhood

If you stood at the intersection of M Street and Wisconsin Avenue NW on a sunny midafternoon, you'd look across a bustling commercial strip. Cars driving west are headed for the Key Bridge, which takes them into the neighborhood of Rosslyn in Arlington, Virginia, or toward Foxhall Road into the very affluent neighborhood of Foxhall-Palisades. To your left and right, ahead of you and behind you, you will see all manner of boutique shops, including Washington, DC's first Apple Store and high-end clothing shops like Abercrombie & Fitch and Calvin Klein. Shoppers with arms filled with bags duck in and out of tiny eateries, and a line three blocks long leads into Georgetown Cupcake, a bakery made famous by the Food Network. Up and down the street, baskets of magenta petunias hang from lampposts, decorating the city street as though it is a suburban outdoor mall. This is the neighborhood of Georgetown, the most exclusive handful of blocks in all of Washington. The shopping caters to the nearby affluent residents of Foxhall, Georgetown, Palisades, and Glover Park, and the neighborhood is a frequent stop for local and national celebrities alike. Georgetown is synonymous with wealth, disposable income, and appearance.

But Georgetown wasn't always *this* Georgetown. In the late 1960s one African American DC resident taking part in a linguistics study commented to his interviewer that "Georgetown was one of the, I don't know, one of the roughest places that– Well, Georgetown and Foggy Bottom are the– of Washington–was one of the roughest neighborhoods that you could come out of. And, uh, and most– like, you live by the sword, you die by the sword, or something of [this nature]. But you had to be strong in order to survive in those places."[1] What happened, to take Georgetown from "one of the roughest neighborhoods you could come out of" to making it synonymous with white people with money to burn? In a word, gentrification.

As in Anacostia, a mix of enslaved Africans and their descendants along with freed Blacks originally populated Georgetown, which had had a sizable African American population since the antebellum period.[2] The city was considered an advantageous port, being situated on the Potomac, and it served as a gateway to shipping west toward Appalachia. By the early 1900s the neighborhood of Georgetown was home to one of the most concentrated African American populations in the city, and it is still home to many Black cultural landmarks, such as Mount Zion United Methodist Church, the first Black congregation in DC.[3]

More than half of the older interviewees quoted in this book were born at Georgetown Hospital, and many of them spent their early childhoods in Georgetown before moving to Anacostia as teens and young adults in the 1940s and 1950s. While this moving process began early in the twentieth century, the 1968 riots accelerated the relocation of a more affluent white population to Georgetown, and the African American residents who had been there were dispersed to other parts of the city, many to the Southeast Quadrant. Legal changes to the neighborhood accelerated this process: during the New Deal, the Old Georgetown Act established Georgetown as a historic district, which caused housing prices to slowly rise. While some Black homeowners were able to benefit from the sale of their appreciated properties, others were pushed out by rising property taxes they could no longer afford.[4] Between 1930 and 1960 the Black population of Georgetown shifted from 30 percent to only 9 percent of the total.[5] By the time of my interviews in Southeast, Georgetown was under 3 percent Black.[6]

This change was mirrored, albeit less drastically, across the District. In the 1970s seven out of ten District residents were African American, and that population was spread throughout the four quadrants.[7] Since the 1970s, however, the population of Black residents in the District has shrunk rapidly, with some quadrants becoming majority white and others experiencing an influx of residents of other ethnicities, such as the growing Hispanic (mostly Salvadoran) population in the Northwest Quadrant neighborhood of Mount Pleasant.[8] As white residents encountered increasingly skyrocketing housing prices in neighborhoods like Georgetown and Dupont Circle, they moved into the eastern neighborhoods of the Northwest Quadrant that the District's Black residents had formerly occupied, pushing those residents further east and south.

Maps which plot the locations and reported ethnicity of 2010 census respondents show sharp divides in populations which correspond to the geographic boundaries within the city. For instance, Sixteen Street NW runs south from the peak of the DC diamond (starting in Silver Spring, Maryland) to the North Lawn of the White House.[9] Once known as the aforementioned "Gold Coast" of Black DC wealth, by 2010 Sixteen Street had become a dividing line in the city.

Figure 2 shows the racial change happening across the district. In 2000, Sixteen Street NW divided areas in the west with a low concentration of African Americans (less than 25 percent) from areas to the east with a high concentration of African Americans (more than 76 percent).[10] Just ten years later, however, the density of African Americans in the east has begun to decrease, with many neighborhoods dropping from 76 percent or higher to 51–75

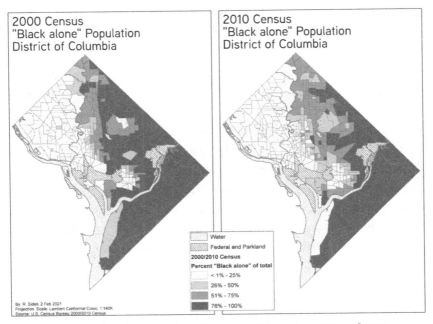

Figure 2. "Black alone" Population, District of Columbia, 2000 and 2010 Censuses. (Maps by Robbie Sidell for ZGeography.com. Used with permission.)

percent and several even down to 26–50 percent. As the white population increased in the far western quadrants and then in the north, then slowly eastward, the District's racial makeup changed as though a fan had begun to open across the District, sweeping first northward and then eastward, and now heading for the south.

Because Georgetown was one of the first places to experience this kind of radical shift from being a center of Black culture to being a place with virtually no Black population, it has unsurprisingly come to stand in for the process of gentrification more generally. "In the eighties, late eighties, early nineties, you can see a change," says Chess, an IT coordinator for one of the elementary schools in Anacostia, who was born in DC in the mid-1950s. "Especially like down on Fourteen Street. You go down there and you be, 'Ooh what's going on', you know. We knew like, uh, Mount Pleasant area, that was Spanish, and the Europeans lived in Georgetown. But we lived in Georgetown at first. And then, uh, gentrification occurred then. Europeans, uh, took over Georgetown, but the early part, like say in the fifties, forties, or thirties, African Americans used to majority live in Georgetown. Then the gentrification happened, and then they moved them out and Europeans took over that area."

Chess is not alone in invoking Georgetown as an example of the racial shift going on in Washington, DC, over the last several decades. For many of the interviewees "Georgetown" has become a metonym—a single place which stands in for the processes that are happening in many places. It is equally unsurprising that Chess invokes Georgetown in racial terms, talking about the "Europeans" who "took over that area" and moved the African American majority out. Throughout most of DC the process of gentrification has meant that white residents have taken over neighborhoods which had a large, if not majority, African American population, so nearly all my African American interviewees frame the process in terms of race.

The increase in the white population in neighborhoods in the Northwest and, increasingly, the Northeast, has changed the demographics of the Southeast Quadrant as well. However, in Historic Anacostia this change was principally one of class rather than race, at least in the initial stages of my research. Yet the discourse surrounding gentrification is so generally racialized that even though gentrification in Southeast had no overt racial component during the time period I consider, residents nevertheless talked about it in terms of race—they made whiteness a proxy for the identity of gentrifier.[11] By talking about whites as the sole actors of gentrification, Anacostia residents discursively erase the existence of African American gentrifiers, casting gentrification as an exclusively racial process. Seeing white people in the neighborhood prompts residents to talk about gentrification, meaning they ignore the presence of new middle- and upper-class African Americans. The ways that residents use personal deixis further accomplishes the racialization of gentrification as they pit the African American "us" against the white gentrifying "them." All this results in further racialization of class.

In this chapter I explore these discourse strategies to uncover the ways in which this racialization results in the characterization of Anacostia as a singular, cohesive Black community, which allows residents to stake claims on the space and make room for middle-class Black investment in ways that are seen as less harmful than in other gentrifying locales. These are the ways in which Anacostia resists being another Georgetown half a century later— centering the African American experience in ways that allow African Americans to broker and control their own power even as the neighborhood begins to change.

### The Discursive Erasure of White People from Gentrification: Three Frames for the White Offensive

"There are certain parts of DC you usedta go and you never"—a bit of nervous laughter—"you only saw Black people," Tracey, a young advisory neighborhood commissioner tells me as we sit across from each other in Anacostia's first coffee shop, located in the Anacostia Arts Center. Each Ward of Washington, DC, is broken into forty advisory neighborhood commissions (ANCs), which were established as part of the DC Home Rule charter. The resident neighbors elect their ANC commissioners, who serve two-year terms as the "neighborhood's official voice" in DC's city governmental structure.[12] "Now you go to those areas, and you're like, 'I don't see any Black people. Like wow, that is crazy, like, I remember when you came here and you only saw 'X' people. Now you come here and you're like, uh, well where like–' Okay? So it has to be drastic for natives."

Tracey is a relative newcomer to Washington, DC. Having finished an undergraduate degree in education in the South, she moved to Washington to work in the public schools. After spending several years teaching, she left for nonprofit work and then moved on to the hyperlocal politics of the ANC. Even as she talks about "the locals," she casts the changes in the wider Washington area in terms of race: places where one doesn't "see any Black people."

The interviews in this book were collected in the early and mid-2010s, after the *Washington Post* identified Anacostia as a hotbed of African American gentrification. During this time census data shows that the African American population in Anacostia stayed relatively steady, dropping only 3 percent, from 98 to 95 percent, in the twenty-five years from 1990 to 2015.[13] During that same time, however, there was a statistically significant decrease in the small white population, from 0.96 to 0.72 percent, which equated to about 40 of the area's approximately 150 white residents. By 2016 the white population had doubled again to around 200.[14] In other words, during the early years covered by my study, white people were not moving into Anacostia and the change in the neighborhood was primarily being driven by young, educated, Black professionals like Tracey, making Anacostia a prime example of Black gentrification. During this time Anacostia also became a location for house flipping, the phenomenon by which houses are bought inexpensively, remodeled, and sold for a profit within a short period of time, usually less than a year. In 2011 house flipping in Anacostia was insignificant; by 2015, flipped houses made up 11 percent of the total homes on the market.[15]

In Chicago's NKO neighborhood, Mary Pattillo notes that "the discourse among black residents concerning the imminence of whites' arrival is more extensive and more telling than their actual presence."[16] I found this to be true in my interviewees' perspectives of Anacostia as well. Even though the racial makeup of Anacostia had not statistically changed during the first phase of my research (2011–13) and the white population had in fact decreased, the talk about who was moving into the neighborhood almost exclusively focused on the presence of whiteness rather than on its socioeconomic shift. This talk took a variety of forms, from wonder at the influx of white people to an attitude of welcome for new racial diversity to thinly veiled (and sometimes not-so-thinly-veiled) derision. Each of these represents a different *frame*—or interpretive schema—through which the presence of whites in Anacostia is viewed and which is evidenced in the ways a given speaker talks about the phenomenon. While most interviewees stuck to a single frame in their discussion of whiteness, a few used several frames, and these took three general valences: white residents as a neutral novelty, white residents as problematic encroachers, and white residents as welcomed diversity.

### Frame 1: "Where Did You Come From?"—Whiteness as Novelty

Tana, introduced in the introduction, is an employee of a local education and economic nonprofit organization in her forties. She related to me a conversation she had with her younger brother, also an Anacostia native:

> You know my brother and I were at a coffee shop on Martin Luther King Avenue, um, it's been more than a year ago. And there were all of these people coming in that were white, okay? So, like I said, when we first moved there [to Anacostia as children] even though it was a changing community I never saw the white people. But we were in there and we're having coffee and these white people are coming in. My brother says to one of the guys, 'Hey what are you doing in here? Where did you come from?" And so the guy said, "Oh I live up the street," and so and so and so and so. And so my brother said, "Who are all these other white people that you're talking to that are coming in here?" And they belonged to some kind of organization, but he said that they all live in Anacostia. So my brother was like, "Wow things are really changing." He said, 'Wow things are really changing, Sis.' I said. "Yeah." I said, "Things are changing."

Tana relates this story in answer to a general question about how the neighborhood is changing, a question which was purposefully left neutral so that interviewees could comment on whatever aspect(s) of the neighborhood's changes they considered to be most salient. While some residents talked about infrastructure changes, such as the introduction of bike share or the opening or closing of grocery stores, most of their answers to this question highlighted what the residents perceived to be changes in the racial makeup of the community.[17]

Tana here uses constructed dialogue to portray her conversation with her brother. Constructed dialogue allows a given speaker to retell their own prior speech or the prior speech of others to describe a given incident, reanimating themselves or another along with whatever impressions they have of the speaker or the speech.[18] By choosing exactly what to repeat, including any additions or subtractions, as well as the intonation and accompanying body language used, the narrator is adding her own interpretation of what about the dialogue matters, why it matters, and how much it matters. In giving her brother an expression of surprise when she voices him saying, "Wow, things are really changing," Tana signals the importance of the influx of white residents as a sign of that change. That Tana chooses this anecdote shows that she shares this opinion; encountering whites in Anacostia is a remarkable turn of events.

The framing of whiteness and white people as foreign to Anacostia is one of the ways that interviewees talked about racial change. It represents the most outwardly neutral way of discussing racial change: for Tana and her brother, while whiteness is remarkable, they do not explicitly state it as good or bad. This "neutral but remarkable" approach is one commonly used by middle-class professional interviewees, particularly those who had also grown up in middle-class families.

Porter, for instance, works in the Smithsonian's Anacostia Community Museum (ACM).[19] The museum, directed by the

Smithsonian's first African American museum director, John Kinard, was opened in 1967.[20]

By the time the ACM opened, Anacostia was already a majority African American neighborhood, and the Black and white demographics only intensified over the next decades. After the 1968 riots the mission of the ACM became unabashedly African American, with the museum organizing Black cultural programming such as Juneteenth and Martin Luther King Jr. Day celebrations on behalf of the entire Smithsonian Institution.[21] For several decades this purpose was more than sufficient. However, as a community begins to change, so too must the programming. Porter argues that "we need to be more diverse. You know because the neighborhood is changing it's not just– it's not all Black. You know this neighborhood is changing so, looking towards the future in terms of programming, we wanna take that into consideration. Certainly take that into consideration."

Like Tana, Porter's discussion of this change is presented in a neutral way. The neighborhood is no longer "all Black," and this reality necessitates change on the part of the museum. Porter points out that this situation is new, and therefore remarkable, but otherwise he does not make an additional value judgment about it. For middle-class residents like Porter and Tana, that the neighborhood's racial makeup is changing is something to be commented on and responded to but not something on which to pass judgment.

This is not the way that everyone views the change in the neighborhood, however. A number of residents, particularly working-class residents and older residents, see the ongoing racial shift as a problem.

Frame 2: "A Subtle Fastness"—Whiteness as Encroachment

"Whites as encroachers" is the second frame through which Anacostians talk about incoming white residents. In this frame, incoming white residents are seen as taking over places that do not belong to them and changing the nature of those places in the process. The theme of worry about the ways that racial change alters a neighborhood is paramount in the comments of many interviewees. This theme principally takes the form of either criticizing what new white residents do or criticizing what the long-term residents perceive they *will* do.

Justin, a teacher at the elementary school in his sixties, points out a concrete way that neighborhoods are changing as the result of what he perceives to be racialized change. "One of the things that, um, um, to me I'm sort of melancholy or sad about is how now that the city has predominately . . . Europeans are coming to the city, or what we say, white folk, that moved into the city—and again, this is all over the country—the changes that are to me most impactful again deal with culture. Deal with the idea that names of neighborhoods are being changed. Uh, so it's not just, um, finance and lack of access for things, but names of neighborhood are changing."

During the course of this project in the mid-2010s, DC neighborhoods were constantly undergoing various kinds of rebranding. Perhaps the most conspicuous of these was naming the neighborhood NoMa (for North Massachusetts Avenue), which became codified in 2011 when the Washington Metropolitan Area Transit Authority changed the name of the New York Avenue/ Florida Avenue/Gallaudet metro station to "NoMa–Gallaudet."[22] New York Avenue, close to Capitol Street, had long been an area of lower-income housing in the Northwest Quadrant, and due to its low property values it was particularly susceptible to the economic pressures that drive gentrification. By the time the metro station name was changed, high-rise condominium buildings were seemingly springing up on every block.

A name change might be considered one way that a neighborhood becomes rebranded—a way of shrugging off whatever associations people have made with a name like "New York Avenue";

a new name opens a means for new interpretations. Justin views this name change as emblematic of white encroachment on the city.

Though this frame was not exclusively used by older and working-class interviewees, it was more common among this group. Chess, the technology aide, is similar in age to Justin and also uses an overt example of this frame. Just after claiming that Europeans "took over" Georgetown, Chess goes on to talk about the ways that the "Europeans" are changing the neighborhoods of Washington, DC, grounding his explanations in his experience as a hired driver for local dignitaries in the 1970s:

> I seen Representative Fauntroy before and I asked him I said, "What is going on?" you know, "Seems like a whole lot more Europeans are coming in and we're being moved out." He said, "It's not only happening here it's happening all over the country." You know, it's a, there's a plan that's gone into effect. And, uh, you can see it. You know, you can see it happening. With you know, they building new establishments and there's people in in in that you haven't seen in the community before a are now in the community, you know. Walking their dogs and stuff like that. And it's– it's almost like: How did this happen? You know, it's like magical. It was a subtle fastness with it, you know. You ain't notice it, then all the sudden it's there. You look up and, "Aw man, what's going on?"[23]

In this excerpt Chess does several things to assert the frame of "whites as encroachers." He describes it as a "plan that's gone into effect." Like Tana, he uses constructed dialogue to express the surprise of people at experiencing new people in their neighborhood, but instead of her "Wow," he voices on behalf of his fellow residents an expression of disbelief: "What's going on?" While he describes this as wonderment—"magical"—and fast, his point is that this is a plan put into action. By framing the quote as having come from DC's congressional representative, Walter Fauntroy, Chess further attempts to legitimize his complaint: this is something that even DC's politicians agree is happening. "In Southeast, Wards 7 and 8, it will get better. It's gonna be better for white– for white people, anyway."

Sally, one of the members of the seniors group, goes even further: "It reminds me of Achebe's *Things Fall Apart*. You know that book? In Africa when the European came and just changed everything. And not necessarily– and usually not for the better."

Sally is far from the only interviewee to connect Anacostia to an African village, a point which I take up more explicitly in the next chapter. Here, however, I wish to point out that the comparison is made not to talk about Anacostia per se but rather to talk about the change in it: in Sally's comparison the white gentrifiers are European invaders, changing an African locale and furthering the frame of whites as taking over.

### Frame 3: "Everybody's Coming Together"—Whites as Diversity

The third frame which interviewees invoke about white gentrifiers depicts incoming white residents as a positive force. A way of rejecting the idea that the neighborhood is all African American (a practice of place discussed more explicitly in the next chapter), this frame paints new white residents as people who are warmly welcomed. Regardless of the kinds of change gentrification brings to a neighborhood, framing white people as a negative force could lead to accusations of racially based hostility. This third frame anticipates such accusations and instead asserts that Anacostia is a place of welcome.

Delores, now in her early sixties, worked most of her life as a receptionist before getting a business degree after retirement. When asked about the ways that the neighborhood was changing, she offered an explanation of some of the rebuilding that is happening on her block: "As you come up on the left-hand side, it's some

houses there, um, that have– is being remodeled. And they occupied by white people. You know that's a good thing. All us supposed to live together. But this, I've never known a white person
to live on Hill Street. Never. So when I walked down the street, I
introduced myself, and spoke with them and everything. Seem to
be nice people. They said they enjoying the neighborhood. I tell
them good."

Delores uses this brief encounter to characterize herself as welcoming—introducing herself to her new neighbors, telling them
it's good that they enjoy the neighborhood. At the same time,
however, this story is set in contrast to the uniqueness of those
neighbors in the first place, that Delores has "never known a white
person to live on Hill Street." Juxtaposing the unusualness of her
new neighbors with her introduction allows Delores to emphasize that she, and by extension all Anacostians, are welcoming of
newcomers.

Delores's welcome is echoed by Jackie, a school administrator
in her fifties who has lived in Anacostia since toddlerhood. Jackie
says, "You know east of the river, it wasn't– it was just, you know,
African Americans. But now, everybody's coming together as one.
So that's a nice change. They come together as one. Instead you
know– you– you right here, then you got Caucasians, um, African
Americans, Koreans. You know– it's– it's a nice change now. It's– I
love it."

Jackie goes out of her way to point out the ways that racial mix-
ing is welcome. She refers to it explicitly as a "nice change" and
emphasizes that the new version of Southeast brings everyone together as one. She emphasizes her racial welcome both by praising
the new diversity and by being inclusive of her immediate audience: given that Asian American residents of Anacostia number in
the single digits, her reference to "Koreans" is likely a reference to
her interviewer, my colleague, Sinae Lee. In referring to Koreans,
Jackie signals welcome of everyone to Southeast: new, old, permanent, or just there to conduct a sociolinguistic interview.

As pointed out earlier, during the course of these interviews the number of white residents in Anacostia only reached 200 in a neighborhood of over 20,000. Talking about whiteness as being a positive force in the neighborhood has two effects. It frames the neighborhood and its residents as welcoming and it serves to still characterize the neighborhood as African American.

Framing, Erasure, and Change

Whether they are a curiosity, a problem, or a welcomed new group, white people are indisputably new to Anacostia. Emphasizing this newness, it turns out, serves an important function when Anacostians talk about gentrification. The ways that Black residents of a gentrifying neighborhood talk about whites in their neighborhood often reflects a sweeping racial lens, even in the face of statistics which might suggest a different, or even nonexistent, racial pattern.

Casting the change in Anacostia, and in DC more broadly, in terms of a shift from African American to white also means that the significance of the presence of middle-class African Americans is diminished. This is an example of what linguistic anthropologists Judith Irvine and Susan Gal call erasure, or the way by which the acknowledgment of a particular distinction serves to obscure the presence of other kinds of distinction.[24] The process of erasure happens in three stages: first the distinction between two things comes to stand for another distinction (iconicity), then the newly iconized distinction obscures within-group distinctions (erasure), and then those distinctions are refracted onto larger and smaller domains (fractal recursivity) so that in the end both small differences and large differences are seen as having the same social meaning.

In the talk of Anacostians, the racial distinction between African Americans and whites comes to be iconic of the distinction between insider and outsider. This iconic relationship between "whiteness" and "non-Anacostian" then obscures differences between African American Anacostians; although a wide range of income levels are represented among the Anacostian Black community, whites are seen as the wealthy newcomers. This in turn casts all African American residents of Anacostia as qualitatively equal in contrast to the whites who are coming in (the erasure process). Then this "Black insider, white outsider" iconization is projected onto DC as a whole.

Thus, when Chess says, "But *we* lived in Georgetown at first" (emphasis added), he projects this iconized racial distinction between African Americans as natives and whites as encroachers onto the broader patterns happening in Washington, DC, not just onto those going on in Anacostia. The "we" puts the entire African American community into one group, erasing differences between African Americans of different socioeconomic statuses, different lengths of residency in Washington, and different home neighborhoods. In so doing it casts the entire process of gentrification in terms of its racial impact and removes any discussion of its socioeconomic drivers.

Anacostia becomes "Black space" through these sorts of erasures. While interviewees, especially older ones, repeatedly brought up the idea of Anacostia as interracial space, in order to counter the prevailing narrative that the rest of the city tells—which equates Blackness with poverty and disorderliness—they seldom mention interracial relations when they discuss the whites presently in the neighborhood. This results in Anacostians characterizing the neighborhood as the place where "we" belong: the historic home of DC's Black residents who have been pushed out of all the other wards.

## Who "We" Is: Unifying the Black Community through Deixis

Gus is a retired truck driver in his midseventies who has lived in Anacostia his whole life, except for a few years of his childhood.

When I interviewed Gus along with Chris, a computer security professional in his thirties, Gus was animated about the issues that concerned him as a neighborhood resident. He talked at length about several changes happening in the neighborhood and for whom those changes mattered. "It will become bad for us," Gus told me. "Us meaning Black folks. It's going– if I move out of Anacostia tomorrow, and want to come back, a house is going to cost me three times as much."

It's not surprising that Gus uses *us* to talk about Anacostians— he is a resident of the community. But in his next comment he makes an explicit connection between the language he uses and the people in the neighborhood, including who will not be served by the changes taking place. The *us* for whom these changes will be bad could be ambiguous: it could mean himself and Chris, or perhaps members of their church, or perhaps Anacostians as a whole. So Gus pauses, taking a moment to be explicit about who he means: "Us meaning Black folks."

The use of deictic positioning to create cohesion among the residents of Anacostia specifically, among DC African Americans more broadly and among the African American community writ large, is an important discourse practice for Anacostians. Deictic words are words which "point": they refer back to real-world antecedents. For example, "this afternoon" has meaning only insofar as the person uttering these words and the person hearing them are experiencing the same day; if "I'll be here this afternoon" is written on an undated piece of paper, the person reading it might not be able to tell exactly which afternoon is meant.

Pronouns, especially first- and third-person pronouns, are deictic markers and have the ability to signal linkages or disunions between groups of people. When someone uses *we* or *us* they are indicating who they view as people who, like themselves, can and cannot be referred to as being a part of the same group. Gentrification at its core is about separating those who belong from those who don't; identifying newcomers and those who are part of the problem versus those who aren't. So this method of grouping serves an important purpose in reinforcing cohesion among neighbors and singling out who does not belong. In contrast, many residents refer to incomers, developers, and others who they don't envision as part of the Anacostian community as *they* and the people they see as members of the community as *we*.

The we is not limited to Anacostians, however. As Gus does, this *we* is often extended far beyond "Anacostian" to mean Black Americans more generally. To briefly revisit a quote in Chess's comments, when talking about his interactions with Representative Fauntroy he offered, "I said what is going on, you know. Uh, seems like a whole lot more Europeans are coming in and we're being moved out." Chess's use of *we* contrasts to "the Europeans" he claims are coming in. When he uses a first-person pronoun he is grouping together all those who are not European and are "being moved out"—in short, the Washington, DC, Black community.

When I asked Sally about the ways that DC more broadly is changing, she offered an explanation of why people didn't cross the river: "DC, now because it's white downtown after dark, well *we're* not down there working like we used to. Or socializing. I think white people have a way of not just making you feel uncomfortable, unwelcome. But there's nothing down there for *us*" (emphasis added).

This *we* that is used throughout the interviews contrasts grammatically with the third-person pronouns *they* and *them*. Sally later opined about what might be happening in the nearby neighborhoods of Capper Homes and Barry Farm, two public housing projects slated for city-funded rebuilding. I discuss these rebuildings in greater depth in the next section, but here I wish to focus on the use of third-person deixis in referring to the developers themselves. "Arthur Capper over here, at– around the Navy Yard? It is beautiful. It is absolutely beautiful over there. And they're threatened wi– They're si– it's a senior home. A senior dwelling and its threatened with– they're threatened with displacement. Not to mention Barry Farms, because of Homeland Security. I don't know where they put Black people. I'm afraid to say that they exterminate them, but I don't know where they put them."

Sally's comments display several obvious instances of third-person deixis. It is important to note, however, that this use takes two forms. In "they're threatened with displacement," the *they're* has an immediate antecedent in "Arthur Capper . . . absolutely beautiful over there." By using "over there" Sally establishes that she is going to talk about something slightly distant, and so she goes on to use the third person. But then she uses a *they* that has no obvious antecedent referent. She next says she doesn't know where *they* put Black people. The *they* here refers to those doing the displacement: the developers, along with those who move into the new developments. This no-antecedent, understood *they* is commonly found in the talk of all interviewees, who cast the encroaching gentrification as something outside the community's control.

Throughout the interviews Anacostians consistently used *we* to bring the entire Black community into the group taking part in the discussions. But making *we* refer to the Black community in turn makes the developers and those moving in as *them*, and not part of *us:* not Anacostian, not Black.

The framing of gentrifiers as white, and the subsequent discursive erasure of Black middle-class gentrifiers, couples with this deictic positioning in powerful ways. Together, these devices position everyone involved in gentrification and in land development as white, which in turn makes Anacostia, and Anacostians, a place and a people which are Black. This makes Anacostia itself Black space, which then has a notable effect on how people racialize issues of displacement, affordability, and class. I turn to these in the next sections.

## Reframing Affordability and Displacement

In September of 2016, DC officials received what some considered wonderful news: they had obtained over $13 million in pre-development funds from the New Community Initiative (NCI) to redevelop the subsidized housing community of Barry Farm.[25] The NCI, which is tasked with replacing public housing with mixed use and mixed income developments at various locations across the United States, considers Barry Farm, with its close adjacency to the Anacostia metro station and the main commercial strip of Anacostia, to be a prime site for redevelopment. Computer-generated renderings of the new community show grinning African American men, women, and children parking bicycles, picnicking, and turning cartwheels on an expansive lawn, while glass-encased buildings glitter in the sunlight behind them.

Barry Farm has its roots in the Reconstruction Era, when in 1867 the Freedmen's Bureau purchased a 375-acre plot of land owned by David and Julia Barry, land that James Van Hook had formerly owned.[26] The farm was sold in one-acre lots to formerly enslaved and born free African Americans: $300 bought a plot of land and enough wood to build a two-room house.[27] Many of the people in the community would work all day across the river as home servants, carpenters, butlers, dockworkers, and the like and then return to Barry Farm to build their homes during the night. This created a thriving community of freed African Americans that existed in stark contrast to the much whiter areas of Washington across the river. The Black residents named this community Hillsdale.

Through the early 1900s the Hillsdale community became increasingly cut off from other parts of the area: Suitland Parkway, to the southeast, and Interstate 295, to the northwest, came through, taking parts of the site in the process. By 1943, when only a few of the original homes still survived and the bulk of the Barry Farm/Hillsdale community had been resold in smaller lots, the National Capital Housing Authority built a 444-unit public housing development on a small portion of the site; other neighborhood building projects took the remainder of the land.

In many ways Barry Farm stands for everything that Anacostia insiders love and outsiders fear. Like other public housing projects around the country, it has seen its share of crime. At the same time, interviewees often cited Barry Farm as a major contributor to the rural, communal nature of Anacostia. For instance, Tana, whose godmother lived in Barry Farm, offers,

> It was almost idyllic. We had great friends. Our parents had friends. And we played without being bothered by people. So it was it was great. People looked out for you. It was great. And so was that– a neighborhood pool that was there. It was a neighborhood pool. It's still there. It's in Barry Farms. So it's in what some people would consider one of the worst neighborhoods in the city but it was the newest pool in the area. So we would walk around there to the swimming pool. No one would bother us. We would get in the pool, swim all afternoon, and get out.

Over the years, however, as the city divested itself of its public housing projects, Barry Farm grew increasingly dilapidated, with houses and yards ill-tended-to. In the mid-2000s, as major changes began in areas of the Northwest Quadrant such as Columbia Heights, the city began to seek investment opportunities for Southeast DC, with a particular focus on Barry Farm. The NCI provided the answer. The plan was to raze the 444 existing units and replace them with new condominiums and townhomes, to comprise 1,400 units total. Among these 1,400 units, 344 were to be subsidized units, and the developer was to build 100 subsidized units "elsewhere in the community."[28]

Building the new units, however, required solving a logistical problem—what to do with the families who already inhabited the units. It meant a mass exodus of people from Anacostia, with over two hundred families needing homes in other parts of the city. Coupled with the knowledge that almost 1,100 of the replacement units would be sold at market rate, and thus unaffordable for the existing residents, the Barry Farm redevelopment project served as a prime example of development excess. After the plan's approval in 2009, as units became empty they were boarded up, resulting in the occupancy rate of the community eventually dropping to less than 50 percent.

This specter of displacement loomed in the background during all of the interviews conducted as part of this project. Every interviewee I spoke with was aware of the Barry Farm redevelopment project, and while not every interviewee discussed it specifically, the idea of people being moved out was consistently referenced. For instance, Gus and Chris brought it up when they discussed Chris's decision as a young adult to move into PG County after he married and had a son. "It's going to be hard getting back in here," says Gus, gesturing through the window of the church eastward, toward Maryland. "If you go out, and I say this, just me, if you go out to Ward 9, which is PG County, it's going to be hard getting back in here." Chris agreed, immediately adding, "Probably like later I'll probably be like, 'Hey I want to get back in,' and you know, I'll be shut out."

One of the principal explanations for the processes and the reasons for gentrification is the rent-gap theory. Analysts argue that the rent gap is the economic driver of gentrification processes and that its effects are cyclical: improvements made in one area mean that surrounding areas become more desirable, which in turn makes the after-improvement value of those areas increase, which in turn makes the difference in price between rents for improved and unimproved properties increase, which in turn makes it more likely that investors will make improvements, and on and on.[29] One result of improved properties, of course, is a general increase in the price of real estate. For people who own real estate this can be beneficial, but in many neighborhoods, especially those with high rental occupancy rates like Anacostia, such a shift means that many of the people who are already there can no longer afford to stay, and those who leave cannot afford to return.

Even while they acknowledge beautiful new spaces that development brings in, some Anacostians focus on who is moved out and consequently keep the discussion about the people who already lay claim to the space. The frame of development as displacement is not limited to lower-income residents either. For instance, Justin, a schoolteacher in his sixties, is careful to talk about some of the positive aspects of development:

> You let things deteriorate, people move out and then our people get displaced and then you you build all of these marvelous new things that you know that could have been there that could have been there before and that people who could have participated in, so you kind of glad that the city is beautiful and there's modernization and there's and things are being built you know y– you you're happy about that and it's becoming a very very beautiful city but folks who really could have appreciated that—because they were here and they wanted that for so long—are no longer here.

Justin juxtaposes the positive aspects of the development—new things that are "marvelous" and "beautiful" and "modernized"—with the fact that people are displaced, emphasizing that those displaced people wanted these same changes and have never had them and now will not be here to enjoy them. This juxtaposition reframes the positive of development as a negative force and one that fails to benefit those who can lay claim to the space.

Tracey, the ANC commissioner, similarly makes it a point to explain that "many native Washingtonians can't afford to come home":

> There are few people you meet who are borned and raised in this city who just absolutely don't wanna be here ever again. They love their city, but I know so many college-educated native Washingtonians who're like, I can't afford to come back home. I can't afford to buy a house in DC in my old neighborhood when they tell you where they lived it's like the homes are a million dollars. It's like

how do you– unless your grandmother you know held onto her
house you have no choice but to leave.

Tracey shifts the framing of who is displaced by pointing out
that the people she is talking about are "college-educated." Because
so much of the discussion about displacement in Washington,
DC, generally, and in Anacostia specifically, centers on housing
that will be affordable to people of lower socioeconomic status,
by bringing up the fact that the people she is talking about are
college-educated, Tracey emphasizes that displacement is a process happening to all Black Washingtonians, not just the poorest
ones. She also explains who is getting to have these new places
when she talks about "native Washingtonians" and people "who
are borned and raised in this city." This casts the people who are
moving in, who can afford the million-dollar houses Tracey describes, as newcomers who do not have the same stake in the city
as the people she is worried about. Displacement, Tracey's framing
says, is not about moving poor people out of dilapidated housing;
rather, it is about newcomers pricing out people who belong in the
city, who ought to have the financial ability to stay where they are.
By focusing on displacement many Anacostians reframe the process of development as a negative force rather than a positive one.

The discourse strategies of framing and deictic positioning
serve to unify the identities of "Black" and "Anacostian" and in
turn to consider developers and incomers as white. As residents
focus on issues of displacement, they carry over this racialization
implicitly and at times explicitly. Sally's statement "I don't know
where they [developers] put Black people" makes this talk about
displacement not just about the replacement of lower-income residents with higher-income ones but about the movement of white
and Black Washingtonians.

Gentrification is an economic issue at its core, and developers
are able to lean on this fact in how they talk about its effects in
order to mask the uncomfortable demographic realities. Yet, when

interviewees connect "displacer" with "developer" and "white," or "displaced" with "native" and "Black," they racialize the process of gentrification. This, in turn, has implications for how socioeconomic class is racialized more generally, which I turn to next.

### Making White People Rich

Framing gentrification as a phenomenon belonging only to white people and unifying the African American community through personal deixis together racialize class as a follow-on effect. When people see gentrified areas as opulent and unaffordable, and those spaces are white spaces, white people become the opulent class; Black people, by contrast, are lower-income. Any process of discourse that erases Black gentrifiers also erases the Black middle class. Discourses of affordability give way to discourses of race: about what change is for and to whom it belongs. This racialization becomes a resource for the ways that Anacostians reject gentrification altogether: it allows Anacostia's status as Black space to be forcefully articulated, while development is seen as an affront to the Black culture with which the space is already imbued.

Several theoretical constructs help explain this process of racializing class difference. The previous sections covered framing, or the process by which a speaker projects a schema of interpretation onto what they say. In talking about class differences between developers and the people who move into developments, speakers change the frame of the discussion from how a development will benefit the community to how it will hurt the community. As this happens, the new development becomes not a positive addition to the neighborhood but one which will displace people from the neighborhood.

The second construct is the act of stance-taking, which is the ways that people signal their relationships toward something or someone (affective stance) or their relationship to what they are saying (epistemic stance).[30] Sociolinguist John Du Bois has perhaps the most famous model of the relationship between and among a specific stance, the thing that stance is taken toward (the stance object), and the person taking the stance. He conceives this process as a triangle, with the stance object at one point of the triangle and the stance-taker and the listener at the other two points. As the two subjects jointly evaluate the stance object, they position themselves relative to it—aligning or disaligning with it—and in turn position themselves with respect to each other.[31] For Anacostians the process of disalignment from the stance object of gentrification—framing it as a racial problem—leads them to in turn align with other neighborhood Anacostians, regardless of the economic status of those other Anacostians. This neutralizes within-group distinctions and reinforces the characterization of the entire neighborhood as Black space.

The act of erasure has further implications for class relationships as well. Just as the erasure of Black gentrifiers classes all gentrification as a white phenomenon, so too does it make the issue of class a white phenomenon: while interviewees often talk about middle-class Blacks as members of the neighborhood community, they regularly omit them from discussions of who is responsible for gentrification (see chapter 2). This absence means that by default white residents are viewed as the sole beneficiaries of development and as the ones who will be able to afford the new housing. This is the last iteration of the process of iconization: "white" becomes synonymous with "gentrifier" and is recursively projected onto other domains, where "white" comes to stand in for "wealthy" more generally. In the previous section I explored how discourses of affordability grow from discourses about whom development should serve, finding that affordability becomes the frame through which these larger questions—of whom development in the neighborhood serves—is interpreted and negotiated. When we explore the interviews for this linkage between affordability and issues of race and racial history, we find many examples, both overt and subtle.

Lucy, a schoolteacher in her midthirties, compares the development happening in Anacostia and just across the river to what she has seen in another major city:

> It kinda reminds me of New Orleans. I lived there for, um, a little bit, but you can have like the poor section of DC, right? And then they'll come and erect this– opulent high-rise condo. And when I tell you opulent, I mean *opulent*. Like the vestibule's made of marble, and blah blah blah, and you will s– And they will come and sit it, right in the middle of the poorest section of the city. You know what I'm saying? And it's almost kind of like a– I don't know. It's like this *energy* I get from it. I don't know if I can really articulate it. It's like a– it's like a snub. It's kind of like, you know, "We're here and we have our money." It's like, "We're flaunting our wealth." Which is– you know, hey, when you work hard for something, you should be able to spend your money however you see fit. But I mean if you are gonna move into a community that has not– like how can you get back to that community or like . . . I just felt like, it's crazy.

Lucy uses several strategies to separate herself from the developers and residents who prefer the "opulent condos." She uses constructed dialogue to speak for them, saying, "You know, we're here and we have our money, we're flaunting our wealth." Her use of the word *flaunting* matches her characterization of the presence of the new developments as a snub.

Like other interviewees, Lucy also makes use of personal deixis to set up the contrast between the regular city residents and those who bring in the opulent new development. She points out that "They'll come and erect this high-rise condo" and "they will come and sit it right in the middle of the poorest section of the city." As in the kinds of personal deixis used by others discussed earlier, she doesn't provide a direct discourse referent for *they*. She simply casts the developers and newcomers as "they," positioning them against an unstated "us" who are being snubbed. In so doing, the "we" becomes the people in the poor section of the city. Recalling the consistency with which residents cast DC's African American community as "we," this contrast has far greater implications than simply comparing developers and the people in the neighborhoods. It racializes these class differences.

Sally, a member of the seniors group, is even more explicit about this connection when she talks about the Duke Ellington apartment building, a historic landmark in the U Street corridor neighborhood, a heavily gentrified and now almost exclusively white neighborhood. Though the area once was the exclusive purview of DC's African American community, now the Ellington building is some of the most exclusive housing in town.[32] "Black people can't afford to live in it. It's not only contradictory, it is– it's an assault. It's a psychological assault. And for them in quotes to 'think that they own it'—the area—and for us not to know how to not just claim it but, um, prove that it's ours? But again that's because we don't know– understand systematic racism. That's the only reason."

Sally, like Lucy, frames the development as an affront to the community but goes even further: "it's an assault." In her view the development is specifically racist in nature. Like Lucy, Sally uses constructed dialogue to mark the words she attributes to the developers and goes so far as to make clear that she is voicing them by saying "in quotes." She then confirms who does own it: the same *us* that Gus and Lucy invoke. In the same us-versus-them contrast Sally positions development as being part of an onslaught offense to the DC African American community, taking away things that belong to the African American community as part of an overall system of racism.

These discussions of development challenge the public narrative that Anacostia needs saving by asserting instead that development actively harms the people of the community, removes their history, and is an affront to their way of life. In addition, that *us* means Anacostia links to the common use of the first person to refer to the DC African American community. It positions the *them*, the developers, as whites and others, those who inhabit the spaces being developed, as Black. In the same way that discourses of developed versus undeveloped space serve to racialize the community, so too do these discourses about development racialize class.

Racializing the differences between insider and outsider, developer and nondeveloper, changes the way that Anacostia itself is imagined. In the discourse of the interviewees, Anacostia is a place which must be protected, and its African American residents are people who must be served. In the eyes of Lucy and Sally, this opposition is straightforward: development is not for "us."

**Conclusion**

If you stood at the intersection of Anacostia's Martin Luther King Avenue and Good Hope Road SE looking east on a sunny afternoon, you'd see a sight quite different from the one you'd see in Georgetown. Most of the buildings are utilitarian: a bank, a pharmacy, a doctor's office, a Social Security office. Signs on the street mark the Anacostia African American Heritage Trail, and the Curtis Brothers Furniture's two-story-tall dining chair is visible in the distance. But little else marks this street as special. There are no hot pink petunias and no bustling shoppers with arms full of the latest brands.

Yet visible signs indicate that some things might be changing in this neighborhood. Down the street, a juice bar, a health food restaurant, and a small organic grocery occupy a handful of spaces that look somewhat similar to places in Georgetown. The new tenants of one of the larger buildings on the street have hung a large banner, proclaiming the home of the Far Southeast Family Strengthening Collaborative, a nonprofit focused on supporting families through economic opportunity and civic engagement. The collaborative's co-tenant is telling: the newest incarnation of Busboys and Poets, the restaurant chain DC immigrant Andy

Shallal started, known for its flagship location in the heart of the gentrified U Street corridor.

Like Georgetown, Anacostia has a long African American history. Blacks and whites lived here, side-by-side if separately, since before the Civil War. Like Georgetown, Anacostia has a long history of freed Black settlement in the community of Barry Farm.

Unlike Georgetown, as the rest of the city changed, Anacostia became the place that African Americans fled to, not where they fled from. Unlike Georgetown, the pace of development here is less rapid—thirty years after Georgetown became a place affluent whites felt was worth going to instead of the rough neighborhood described in 1968, Anacostia's main drag only recently has acquired a bookstore and an independent coffee shop. It still has only a handful of sit-down restaurants. Even Starbucks, often seen as a key gentrification harbinger, has taken its time crossing the river.[33]

All this means that Anacostians have had the time to observe what is happening in the rest of the city and to decide through which lens they will view those changes. That lens is predominately a racial one. Framing whiteness in the neighborhood as unusual and remarkable simplifies all of the changes which are taking place into racial ones—iconizing gentrification as a process that white people "do" to Black people. At the same time, the occasional framing of white residents as adding to diversity ensures that even while gentrification is being firmly viewed through a racial lens, opposition to it is not about being hostile to whites.

The use of personal deixis unifies the "Us meaning Black folk," as Gus puts it, and contrasts Anacostians to an antecedent-free *they* that stands in for the developers, urban planners, and movers-in. Doing so implicitly sets up a racial contrast which both excludes Black residents from being the developers and characterizes those involved in the processes of changing the neighborhood as white.

Once this schema separates the Black residents from the white developers, and once the entire phenomenon of gentrification is iconized as a white phenomenon, the racial distinction is recursively pushed onto other domains, so that unaffordability and higher socioeconomic class become seen as primarily white. Meanwhile, the framing of new white residents as a welcome addition to increase the diversity of the neighborhood allows residents to take up stances which are anti-gentrification without seeming overtly anti-white.

Preserving Anacostia's characterization as a Black community is important within the greater history of Black migration across the city. If the same economic hand of fate which swept Black people out of Georgetown continues its sweep across the city, the change to the Southeast Quadrant isn't far behind. Discourses which turn gentrification into a purely racial phenomenon obscure any role that Black middle-class Washingtonians may play in these patterns of change. It effectively takes them out of the problem of gentrification, implicitly countering any claim that gentrification is a class issue.

Often, economic explanations for gentrification mask more racial, and racist, motivations for change, such as when developers appeal to "property values" without attending to the fact that disparities in property values often fall along racial lines. Even more troubling is that the residents themselves often repeat these same explanations, so that the process is only explained in terms of the flow of money.[34] Here, however, can be seen exactly the opposite: both overtly and covertly, residents reframe the discussion and shift its focus from economics to race. This rejection of the broader narrative about gentrification stakes a definitively Black claim on Anacostia—implicitly protecting it from becoming another metonymic "Georgetown."

## Notes

1. Fasold, *Tense Marking in Black English;* Kendall and Farrington, CORAAL DCA, participant se2ag3m1.

2. In 1810 the population of Georgetown was 35 percent Black, with two-thirds being enslaved persons; by the advent of the Civil War, though the population had dropped to 22 percent Black, only a third of those Blacks were enslaved. K. Smith, *Washington at Home.*

3. K. Smith, *Washington at Home.*

4. K. Smith, *Washington at Home.* This happened throughout the Washington area in the 1940s through 1970s, leading to a great deal of the suburban flight.

5. K. Smith, 31.

6. Open Data DC, "Demographic ACS Characteristics 2011 to 2015," accessed August 2021, Opendata.dc.gov; US Census Bureau, "ACS 5 Year Estimates 2016," Census.gov, accessed August 2021.

7. Morello and Melnick, "District Grows Younger and More White, Census Statistics Show," *Washington Post*, June 12, 2013.

8. Modan, *Turf Wars.* Modan provides a discourse analytic perspective onto the shift in this neighborhood.

9. Graham, *Our Kind of People*; Robinson, *Disintegration.*

10. A quirk of DC geography is the naming of its numbered streets: in most places in the District, historically the numbered streets did not include the ordinal indicator, such that the sign might read "16 St NW." While this practice has changed as street signs have been updated, these ordinal-free signs can still be found throughout the city and many Black Washingtonians, particularly older ones, do not use the ordinal in the name of the street as a way of signaling their native Washingtonian identity. In this book I follow this linguistic practice of place, especially for streets which have traditionally been home to the most vibrant DC African American populations, Sixteen and Fourteen Streets NW.

11. Modan, *Turf Wars*; Lou, *Linguistic Landscape.* Other linguistic studies of gentrification show that the demographic shifts taking place are typically described in terms of white residents replacing residents of color.

12. City of Washington, DC, Advisory Neighborhood Commissions.

13. Emily Wax, "'Gentrification' Covers Black and White Middle-Class Home Buyers in the District," *Washington Post*, July 29, 2011.

14. Urbandata.dc; District of Columbia Planning Office, DC State Data and opendatadc.

15. DataLensDC, https://www.datalensdc.com/dc-property-flipping.html.

16. Pattillo, *Black on the Block.* In allied work, sociologist Mary Pattillo explores what she terms "Black gentrification" in the North Kenwood–Oakland (NKO) neighborhood in Chicago. She similarly finds that affluent

Black residents moving into NKO, as well as their longtime resident neighbors, talk about gentrification in terms of it being a "white offensive" (129).

17. Su and Wang, "Three Ways Bikeshare." A bike-sharing program, Capital Bikeshare, opened in 2010. Operated by Motivate, which owns bike-sharing programs in cities across the country, the service offers short-term rental bikes throughout the city. Throughout the 2010s the service expanded into the Northwest, Southwest, and Northeast Quadrants. However, the growth has been very uneven: areas like Anacostia, which have the lowest percentage of white population, on average have only a quarter as many bike stations.

18. Tannen, *Talking Voices*. Tannen provides a detailed explanation of constructed dialogue in interaction.

19. Many of the landmarks in Anacostia are all but impossible to obscure in a work of ethnography. For instance, it is important and remarkable that Our Lady of Perpetual Help Church was the first African American Roman Catholic congregation in Washington, so to keep its name anonymous would mean omitting a crucial part of the historical narrative. Similarly, the Smithsonian Anacostia Community Museum is an important cultural touchpoint in the neighborhood that could not easily be referred to pseudonymously without making clear exactly which institution is being referred to. For this reason I have chosen to not use pseudonyms for some of the neighborhood institutions; instead I do not reveal the exact nature of my interviewee's relationship to them so as to preserve the interviewee's anonymity.

20. Smithsonian Anacostia Community Museum, "Making of a Museum."

21. Smithsonian Anacostia Community Museum, "Making of a Museum."

22. Mark Berman, "New York Ave. Metro Station Becomes No-Ma Stop," *Washington Post Local*, 2012.

23. Walter Fauntroy was DC's first elected congressional representative after the Home Rule Act passed in 1970. He served 1971–91.

24. Irvine and Gal, "Language Ideology."

25. Predevelopment funding are the loans and grants given to an organization to facilitate the development of a proposal and usually covering items such as legal fees, site surveys, architectural renderings, and environmental impact studies. Their use signals the funding organization's commitment to facilitating the project to be proposed (nhc.org).

26. Hutchinson, *Anacostia Story*.

27. Amos, "Ten Strong"; K. Smith, *Washington at Home*; Fitzpatrick and Goodwin, *Guide to Black Washington*.

28. New Communities Initiative, "Barry Farm Redevelopment Plan."

29. Palen and London, *Gentrification*; N. Smith, "Gentrification and the Rent Gap."

30. Johnstone, "Community and Contest." I rely in part on the definition Johnstone provides: "Stance is the methods, linguistic and other, by which interactants signal relationships with the propositions they utter, and the people they interact with" (31). See also Kärkkäinen, *Epistemic Stance,* for explanations of epistemic and affective stance.

31. Du Bois, "Stance Triangle"; Johnstone, "Community and Contest."

32. At the time of this writing a one-bedroom, one-bathroom apartment in the Ellington building is listed for over \$2,600 per month, more than 25 percent above the DC median income of \$2,060.

33. The first standalone Starbucks location in Anacostia was slated to open inside Maple View Flats, a new affordable-housing apartment complex that opened in 2017. After construction was halted by protesters in 2018, construction slowed. The Starbucks ultimately opened there on May 22, 2020, after a nearly three-year delay.

34. Pattillo, *Black on the Block*; Prince, *African Americans and Gentrification.*

# Chapter 2

# "Beauty within Itself"

Circulating Insider Discourses to
Counteract Outsider Views

I open my computer in my office in Tennessee, five hundred miles from my research site, type into the search bar "Anacostia, DC," and immediately receive a carefully curated barrage of news. Many items relate to urban development—chronicling the creation of the new Eleventh Street bridge park, describing home prices, featuring new day care facilities. Buried among all these stories, however, is a *Politico* profile of Ryane Nickens, a Howard University–educated Ward 8 resident.[1] She is the founder of the TraRon Center, an organization dedicated to assisting communities in preventing and healing from gun violence. The center is named for her two siblings, Tracy and Ronnie, both of whom were killed in shootings in the District. Nickens, as a lifelong east-of-the-river resident, says that she "could have moved to a different part of the city. But this is home. Ward 8 is where I stay. Where I buy a house. It's easy to get up and leave. But if all of us get up and leave, our children and our young people don't have the representation that they can make it out of their circumstances."

Accompanying the article is a dark photo of Nickens, standing on a rainy day in front of a set of newer, brightly painted rowhouses that I recognize as being part of a development near the Anacostia Community Museum. The bright colors of the rowhouses seem to contrast with Nickens's warm-looking coat and umbrella—the photo seems to signify both new growth and stormy weather.

Profiles like Nickens's tell two stories. One is that Southeast DC is the place where Ryane Nickens wants to stay, to represent resilience to her neighbors and children. The other is that Southeast is the place where Tracy and Ronnie were killed. News stories like this one underscore the desire of new movers and shakers to open services that will better the community by emphasizing how some have returned to the neighborhood where they grew up. At the same time, they perpetuate the stereotype that East of the River is riddled with poverty and gang violence.

DC's newspaper of record, the *Washington Post,* and the African American community newspaper, the *Washington Times,* have historically been littered with examples of the ways that outsiders discuss Anacostia. Articles going back to the 1960s and 1970s call it the "slums," the "model of all that is wrong with urban living," and the "city's basement."[2] Articles in the 1990s still refer to it as a "forgotten" area in an "oft-neglected ward" and in the 2000s as a "scarred piece of land."[3] Even articles that ostensibly intend to portray the neighborhood as "friendlier" and highlight its culture call it "third-world in feel."[4]

A nonspecialist might call these circulating ideas the general "discourse" about Anacostia, and they would be correct. *Discourse,* as sociolinguists define it, refers to a broad set of linguistic and nonlinguistic practices which work to create meaning beyond the level of the sentence, encompassing things such as interaction, narrative, and organization of speech. In the words of linguist Norman Fairclough, discourse is "more than *just* language use, it is language use, whether speech or writing, seen as a type of social practice."[5] The social practice aspect of discourse means that each of these linguistic practices are ways speakers create social meaning and tie their talk to their social identities. Discourse, therefore, is one of many ways in which Black speakers have a means of marking ourselves as culturally Black. For example, if a Black speaker uses the Black discourse strategies of *signifyin'* and *marking*, which involve ritual wordplay and insult but which are highly culturally constrained to produce interspeaker closeness, they may well be misunderstood by a white speaker who does not have access to the same discourse repertoire (see chapter 3).

The ways by which speakers employ discourse practices can be particularly situated within a culture even if similar practices are used by other groups. In chapter 1, for instance, we see the workings of framing and deixis as part of discourse, functioning to unravel the differentiated, and racialized, social positioning of Anacostia residents versus outside gentrifiers. It is not that white speakers do not use deixis and framing as strategies, but that these two strategies are available to make particular kinds of raciospatial assertions which reinforce Black cultural identity in Anacostia. Each of the linguistic practices of place explored in this book are acts of discourse, whether reframing (chapter 1), responding to positioning (chapter 2), style-shifting (chapter 3), or imagining larger frameworks of Black success (chapter 4). In this chapter I focus on the function of "lowercase-d" discourse in responding to what James Gee calls "Big-D Discourses": the ways that people, places, and things get recognized as having socially significant identities.[6] The ways that we talk about a particular place or a particular set of people in turn characterize that place or set of people in ways which reify their identities across time. The Big-D Discourses in circulation about Anacostia provide a particular way of interpreting the neighborhood: that it is crime-ridden, poverty-stricken, urban, dirty, and backward.

Big-D Discourses serve to characterize a neighborhood in the minds of outsiders in ways that profoundly impact those who live in that neighborhood. Because these Discourses are in consistent circulation, when residents talk about their neighborhood they are implicitly rebuffing them, responding to the ways that others characterize the neighborhood even when their immediate audience is merely an interviewer who is asking them to talk about the neighborhood itself.

One way of understanding these responses is through *positioning*, which Rom Harré and Fathali Moghaddam define as explaining how "people use words (and discourse of all types) to locate themselves and others" and to "ascribe rights and claim them for ourselves."[7] We can envision the ways that people position themselves and others via discourse as falling along two axes: the positioning of self and others, and the degree to which these positions respond to other positions. In self-positioning a person positions themself without responding to another position. This self-positioning, however, may also occur in response to the ways that someone else has already positioned them. This latter type of positioning, forced self-positioning, is a person's response to the ways others have positioned them.[8]

The Big-D Discourses in circulation about Anacostia allow outsiders of the neighborhood to position it: they form something of an institutional discourse through which people interpret Anacostia, Ward 8, and Southeast DC.[9] Thus, stories like Nickens's, which on the surface are stories about triumph and people staying in Southeast, ultimately rest on the assumption that Southeast is already a place of crime—her triumph is a self-positioning in response to the assumed criminality present in the Discourse.

Each and every time a resident talks about the neighborhood they must deal with this interpretive frame: to talk about Anacostia is to somehow confront the Discourse of disarray imposed on it. When residents on occasion take this Discourse as true, they tend to do so in an effort to justify capital investment in it or explain their reasons for moving away from it. However, for Anacostia residents most of the time talking about their home means rejecting this Discourse and instead emphasizing the reasons they live where they do. This chapter looks at the many ways that residents resist these Discourses and the ways that this forced-self positioning leads to new Big-D Discourses that affirm the neighborhood's value.

Despite the pervasiveness of these negative characterizations, residents rarely address them overtly and only a handful of such moments occurred among the interviewees in this project. Kiesha, for instance, a teacher at the local elementary school, says, "Southeast, period, has always been known for 'You don't wanna go to ward– go to Southeast, that's the bad part of the city.' That is been known for that, especially Ward 8. That, you know, the crime."

Like others discussed in chapter 1, Kiesha uses constructed dialogue to put words into the mouths of others. This constructed dialogue serves both to reflect the comments that others have made about Southeast—pointing out the ways that the rest of the city feels about the community—and also to point out that the people who say such things are outsiders passing information to one another. While the constructed dialogue is an indirect way of talking about these opinions, she states the opinions openly and directly, saying, "Here is the opinion that others hold."

More common than the way Kiesha comments, however, is the use of outsider opinion as either an explanation for the lack of amenities in the neighborhood or as a way of showing change in a personal relationship to the neighborhood. Leona, an administrator in Kiesha's same elementary school, observes that a frequent sight in the rest of the District is almost never seen in the Southeast Quadrant:

Well I've been hearing some wonderful things about those trucks. They have some good food out there, you know. So I been planning to check them out, but they just don't come down to this area. This part of the city. They don't come down, because some of these– some of these companies are afraid to come in Southeast, you know. Because, you know, Southeast, this part of the country has always had a reputation of being the bad part of the city.

Leona explicitly acknowledges that Southeast has a "reputation of being the bad part of the city," but she uses this acknowledgment as part of a larger explanation for why food trucks, nearly ubiquitous in the Northwest Quadrant, don't show up. The appeal to Southeast's reputation, along with stating that the companies are "afraid to come in," suggests that the reputation is not justified.

Similarly, residents use overt mentions of the neighborhood's reputation to set up a change of heart on their part, as Robert does. Robert, a man in his early forties, is a Washington native who moved to Southeast as an adult. He became active in the community nonprofit sector, and the week before I interviewed him he had joined an organization involved in building a major new park and recreation area on the river. "I grew up in Northeast DC," he says. "Even then there was this barrier between Northeast DC and Southeast DC. And I didn't grow up in a rich part of town, but it was still—in our perspective—better than Southeast DC. Like Southeast was, like, that bad place."

Robert acknowledges the opinion that Southeast is "like, that bad place" as a setup for him to juxtapose the opinion he had growing up against the fact that when he moved to Anacostia he discovered that his neighbors were friendly and that it is a very desirable place to live.

In the handful of times that interviewees explicitly addressed the reputation of the neighborhood, they usually did so to explain why others, especially whites, do not wish to come into the neighborhood, and they usually follow their overt acknowledgment of how that reputation positions the neighborhood with an explanation of why the neighborhood's reputation is undeserved. Most of the time, however, the Discourses surrounding Anacostia and the Southeast Quadrant serve as background for other kinds of discussions. They are not explicitly addressed or talked about in conversation but rather are assumed to be understood by the audience. Despite the fact that they do not explicitly acknowledge them, residents consistently respond to the ways outsiders position their neighborhood when those outsiders describe its history and its current state.

This chapter explores the specific ways that Anacostians' talk rejects these Big-D Discourses of crime, filth, incivility, and poverty. Instead of responding directly to these characterizations, residents change the frame, or interpretive schema, of the neighborhood: they emphasize its safety, beauty, close-knittedness, and socioeconomic diversity as a means of implicitly countering the ways that outsiders position their neighborhood. They re-envision the neighborhood as safe, beautiful, and desirable and, in turn, implicitly suggest that none of these positive attributes are lacking merely because the neighborhood is predominately Black. These repositionings are insider discourses: the agreed-upon ways of talking about and interpreting the neighborhood that are in wide circulation but only among the residents and stakeholders in the community itself. These insider Discourses also convey wariness about how the neighborhood is changing—positioning newcomers as disrupting the close-knit nature of the neighborhood and encroachers on the beauty that the neighborhood residents enjoy.

## "People Had All Kinds of Fruit Trees": Rejecting Urban Filth through Discourses of Beauty

Martin Luther King Boulevard, the main street of Historic Anacostia, is situated at the bottom of a large hill which leads up to historic Fort Stanton, a defense outpost the Union Army used during the Civil War. From Fort Stanton one can look back across the Anacostia River toward downtown DC, with its magnificent vistas of the Capitol Dome, the Washington Monument, and the lights of the city. This view is widely regarded as one of the best in Washington, and every year watching the July 4th fireworks on the National Mall from the steps of Our Lady of Perpetual Help, the Black Catholic church at the top of the hill, is a favorite moment for Anacostians and non-Anacostians alike.

One way residents are force-positioned is through the characterization of the neighborhood as dirty, ugly, and ill-kept. As a result, in many interviews the residents countered this positioning by talking about Anacostia's beauty—the parks, the view from the hill, the ways it used to be very rural. This emphasis serves two purposes: one, it rejects the forced positioning of the neighborhood as dirty and ugly by asserting the ways in which it is not; and two, it repositions Anacostia as an attractive place to live. Both counter the broader characterization and subtly justify the residents' concern that other Washingtonians will want to move in.

Among Mr. Moore's reasons for moving across the river was his appreciation for the fact "that if I wanted a garden in my yard, I knew I could have a garden in my yard." In talking about his garden, Mr. Moore contrasts it to his own impression of the rest of Washington as "dirty" and "nasty," exactly the kinds of impressions of Anacostia that circulate among outsiders. He inverts the standard Discourse: in his view, the rest of DC is dirty and Anacostia is attractive and natural.

An excellent example of both of these Discourses comes from Gus, one of the interviewees from Our Lady of Perpetual Help. When discussing the neighborhood he points out that the church sits on

> the tallest place in this– in Anacostia. You look up, there's the church. You look up, there's the church. You look up here. You know, you look up. You come across the bridge, either one of those bridges down there, and you can look to your immediate left or right and you see it. There it is, right there. And then when the fall comes and the trees bare their– I mean, give way, give their leaves back to the earth . . . You can really see it. Beautiful up here. You want to come up here and stand and just look over. Just look over the city . . . This is what you want. This is what we have. Beauty within itself. That's what the– you know, that's what this is up here. Beauty. I love it up here.

Gus emphasizes the natural beauty of Anacostia: he mentions the trees as well as the views. Focusing on the trees emphasizes

Anacostia as a natural rather than urban space, and contrasts it with the view of downtown one can get by climbing the Fort Stanton hill. That Anacostia is a place of nature is particularly important for the older interviewees, who often emphasize the ways that Anacostia was not a bustling urban center when they grew up in the 1930s, 1940s, and 1950s. When talking about the Anacostia in which they grew up, the residents emphasize how the neighborhood defied expectations of what urban life should look like.

"It was rural," says Carol, a member of the Anacostia Community Center Elders Group, who is a lifelong resident of the neighborhood and worked as an administrator in the local schools.

> We didn't have roads and stuff. We– right, we had to walk on the dirt roads until they came over and, you know, we had streets and roads. Because there are some streets that are not even streets anymore because the, um, woods have taken them over. Like up here, um, across from the Anacostia museum, used to be a street. Because it used to be homes back in those woods that are not there anymore because the woods have taken over and the streets are gone. So it was basically a rural area. People had all kinds of fruit trees in they yards. They had chicken and, I mean it—just like a little farmhouse and houses and everything. So really. They had an outhouse. Over time it changed as it became civil– uh, quote-unquote civilized.

Like Mr. Moore, Carol draws an image of old Anacostia as a place where people cultivated food (fruit trees) and had other hallmarks of country life, such as chickens. She ends by talking about how the neighborhood became "quote-unquote civilized."

The emphasis on Anacostia's natural beauty and rurality press back against some of the impressions that outsiders often have of Anacostia, particularly that it's a site of urban blight. By emphasizing its natural beauty and its historically rural character, older Anacostians reject the notion of Anacostia as urban, and in so doing they subtly reject some of the other aspects of its urban characteristics, such as poverty and crime.

This rejection can be seen most powerfully in the final line of Carol's quote, a single sentence that goes a long way toward exhibiting her stance toward the disappearance of the ruralness of her youth. She begins by simply saying, "It changed as it became civilized," but then she backtracks. To say that Anacostia changed to become civilized would imply that Anacostia was not civilized during the time she is describing. So she stops herself midsentence and says instead, "quote-unquote civilized." By setting off *civilized* in this way she distances herself from the word. The "quote-unquote" marks the term *civilized* as not Carol's term but a term that someone else is applying. By setting off the words in this way Carol is able to appropriate them while also calling into question whether "civilization" is what has happened. While one might consider "civilization" to exclude chickens and foxes and outhouses, Carol is pointing out that this rural, old Anacostia was civilized too.

### The Metaphor of Smallness

"Anacostia is a relatively small area," says Gus. "All of Southeast is not Anacostia. Anacostia starts as soon as you come across the bridge—either the Eleven Street or the other bridge, and it starts there. Runs up Fairlawn Avenue to Anacostia High School, up Minnesota to Good Hope Road. Up Good Hope Road. It encompasses all of that. That's Anacostia."

For residents of Anacostia, rejecting outsider positioning of their neighborhood includes not only the discourses about the ways the space should be characterized but also how people talk about the physical space itself. When I, as an outsider to the neighborhood and a relative newcomer to Washington, DC, ask about the community, native Anacostians often make sure that I have

not fallen into the trap that many other Washingtonians, especially Northwest Quadrant dwellers like myself, do by telling me
that when other DC residents say "Anacostia," they often use it as
a synecdoche for the entire Southeast Quadrant, which includes
two wards and over forty neighborhoods. They are quick to point
out that Anacostia itself is quite small, as Gus does when he names
the roads that mark Anacostia's borders. Many of the interviewees
in this work emphasized that while Anacostia is the most famous
of the neighborhoods east of the river—because of its place in history and the name it shares with the river—the actual neighborhood is less than 1.5 miles square.

Talking about boundaries emphasizes the nature of the space
and demarcates a specific community that is separate from the
remainder of DC. At the time of these interviews, the population
of DC was just barely 600,000, keeping it out of the top twenty
most populous cities in the United States. The broader metropolitan area houses almost twice as many people, making Washington
seem like a larger metropolis than it actually is, but the District
itself, with its ten-mile-square border and height-restricted buildings, is small in many senses of the word. Within it, discourses
of size and population are continually refracted onto the space of
greater Washington to emphasize the natures of different communities in contrast to one another. As this refraction takes place,
common themes emerge. As with talk about the physical beauty
of the space, talk about physical smallness is one way in which
residents reposition the community as attractive, as ANC commissioner Tracey does: "I wanted to move here, and move to Anacostia, because I thought, 'Oh this is great. I'm in DC but I feel like
I'm in a small community in Anacostia.' Love it, yes. We have our
own entrance– You know, when you're in Anacostia, it doesn't matter where you drive into– into this ward. You know you're here."

The idea of smallness is reflected in Tracey's explicit reference
to a "small community," but she takes it a step further than Gus in
talking about the boundary as constituting welcome: "You know

you're here." Talking about the community as small, therefore, serves to emphasize the ways in which it is a *community*, a place that is clearly bounded and that greets you when you arrive. In so doing, "community" stops marking only the physical space; instead it projects social cohesiveness onto that space. Small size becomes a proxy for close-knittedness, and the physical smallness serves as a metaphor for how the community members are connected.

### "I Feel Warm Here": Rejecting Crime and Disarray through Discourses of Close-Knittedness

Another very common device creates community close-knittedness, especially among older speakers, namely the comparison of Anacostia to an African village. Dianne Dale, a local community historian whose work on Anacostia is embedded throughout the historical archives about Anacostia as well as in several books about Black Washington, titled her collection of oral histories about Anacostia *The Village That Shaped Us,* calling to mind this image. Dale suggests in the foreword the urgency of recording this "villageness" as the neighborhood changes:

> Our communities are fast disappearing along with our history because we haven't told it to our children and haven't recorded it. We need to write it down. Each story is important to making it more complete. If we all tell our stories, short or long, we have another thread running through the tapestry that depicts our life here. We must mark the place where it happened and tell how it happened in our own words, as we lived it, one by one, or it will be gone forever. We are the last generation to know it.[10]

Dale's book focuses on the former residents of Hillsdale, the Freedmen's Bureau–funded community formed out of the sale of John Barry's farm. Her interviewees emphasize the same themes of close-knit ties that abound in this project's interviews as well.

Interviewees compare Anacostia to a village both implicitly, in the ways that they talk about the community, but also often explicitly, as in the case of Sally, a member of the seniors group I interviewed in 2015. A retired social worker in her seventies who has lived in Anacostia her whole life, Sally describes Southeast DC's change as "making her cry":

> It reminds me of [Chinua] Achebe's *Things Fall Apart*. Uh, in Africa when the European came and just changed everything, and not necessarily—and usually not for the better. In Barry Farms, it was like a community, and the neighbors parented you . . . Barry Farms was like an African village. I didn't know that until I went to Senegal, and I saw the comparison. The similarity. Whereas— um, a– because there they lived in compounds, like, and– Barry Farms you socialized in the alley. So it was a back door and you all came out there and you played what have you. And any adult had the right to correct you. That's very African, even today.

Sally extends the metaphor of an African village by making specific analogies to smaller aspects of the Anacostia space, which is another example of the ways that discourses about community are fractally recursive. In Sally's description each aspect of the village has a parallel in Barry Farms: the compounds become the alley; the back doors become the ways that people enter into the communal space and where any adult can reprimand a child.

Most elder interviewees brought up the metaphor of Anacostia as an African village. In emphasizing the "village-ness" of Anacostia, the interviewees reject the notion that people in Anacostia do not look out for one another. In addition, the village frame serves to reject the concept of Anacostia as urban space.

### Knitting the Neighborhood

"You know, when I tell people I grew up in Anacostia they look concerned," Tana tells me. Having just finished discussing some of the ways that others see Anacostia, she goes on to discuss how her experience fails to mesh with what she hears from others: "You know and I tell them, believe it or not my childhood was almost idyllic you know, it was almost idyllic, we had great friends, our parents had friends and we played without being bothered by people, so it was—it was great. People looked out for you—it was great."

When outsiders characterize Anacostia, they often imply the neighborhood is in disarray both physically and societally—crime-ridden and unsafe. Residents explicitly reject this positioning by emphasizing the neighborhood's safety; they also implicitly reject it by talking about the neighborhood's close-knit nature. Positioning the neighborhood as a place of close ties allows residents, especially middle-class residents, to subtly talk about the changes occurring there.

Robert grew up with the impression Southeast was "that bad place," but he found something different when he actually moved in:

My mom—she lived over in Southeast. My parents are separated. I stayed with my dad. So when I would go visit, I would go visit her in Southeast. And I'm like– when we had to catch the train over there, I didn't wanna go. Cause I'm like, I'm s– sc– ya know I don't want anything to happen. Um, and it wasn't because of experiences. It was just because, you know, a lot of the images that I'd been shown, things that I'd been told, about you know, the Southeast. And as an adult, once I've lived over here, and experienced the people? Like, I don't wanna leave.

Robert presents his early impressions of Southeast primarily to juxtapose them against his later understanding: he rejects the "images that I'd been shown" and "things that I'd been told" in favor of his actual experiences. This strategy is especially powerful because when Robert acknowledges his initial negative opinion of Southeast, he is aligning with others who hold the same opinion. When he instead winds up having overwhelmingly positive experiences in the neighborhood as an adult, he suggests that just as his opinion of the neighborhood is able to shift, so too would theirs, a point he goes on to make explicitly: "Especially when folks are coming over to the city, I want them to have a positive experience. So that they can see like, ya know, this is what the ward really is."

What the ward really is, Robert suggests, is the people and how they live together and look out for one another. His linking of the two examples echoes Tana's point. Emphasizing the ways in which Anacostians are known for looking out for one another is a strategy that is not limited by age cohort either. Sally, in discussing the ways that Southeast differs from Northwest, offers this: "[On] the subway a man seldom off– gives you a seat. But on the bus, the black– the buses coming here become Black as on Pennsylvania Avenue I think. And I don't care how dirty a man is from working in construction or what have you, he's going to offer you his seat. That– that politeness. I feel warm in Southeast. I wouldn't live anyplace else."

Sally frames her comfort in terms of the geography itself: the Pennsylvania Avenue bridge sits approximately a mile east of the Eleventh Street bridge and brings people into the eastern side of the Southeast Quadrant. She identifies "crossing the bridge" as being the place where a man will offer his seat. It is important to note also that Sally describes this as being part of the shift in racial demographics: it is not only that the buses cross Pennsylvania Ave but that the buses "become Black." Like the interviewees in the previous chapter, Sally connects safety and politeness with Blackness and inverts the characterization of the neighborhood as being in disarray. Instead, Sally says, the Black buses are where politeness happens. They become the desirable space.

Emphasizing the close-knittedness of the neighborhood is a way to reject the forced-positioning of the neighborhood as an undesirable locale. In many interviewees' responses Anacostia changes from a place of crime to a place where "people looked out for you" (Tana) and where no matter "how dirty a man is . . . he's going to offer you his seat" (Sally). They reposition the neighborhood as safe, comforting, and, importantly, desirable.

### "Everybody Had a Mother and a Father": Rejecting Poverty through Discourses of Class Diversity

The final Big-D Discourse that residents combat is that Southeast is the impoverished part of DC. While the strong correlation between race and class in Washington can result in the erasure of the Black middle class in the discussion of gentrification, Anacostians often invoke the long history of Black middle-class Anacostians when they talk about their neighborhood. Beginning with the freed Blacks who purchased plots of land from the Freedmen's Bureau to build Hillsdale after the Civil War, Anacostia has always been a place where Black people were homeowners who experienced American prosperity. That Anacostia, and the District of Columbia more broadly, has a sizable population of affluent Blacks is a point that many of my interviewees bring up. For instance, Lucy, an elementary schoolteacher, contrasts the District with other places she has been:

> One thing about DC—and I didn't realize it until I started living other places—is that not only do we have a large number of African Americans in one city, but just kind of like the, um, I guess the economic makeup of that amount of African Americans in one place where you do have, um . . . abject poverty but you have like a lot of affluent African Americans, and when I've lived in other places usually the African American communities were the poorest in those communities. And that's it. You didn't really see too many, you know, African Americans who were affluent or, you know, involved in, um, politics.

The affluence of the upper-class Black families who lived in Washington, DC's Gold Coast (upper Sixteenth Street NW) in the

1960s, 1970s, and 1980s gave the city its reputation for African American affluence. When wealthy Blacks moved from DC into Prince George's County, that county became the largest concentration of Black wealth in the United States. This reputation of DC as a bastion of Black wealth runs entirely counter to the Discourses currently in circulation about DC, Southeast DC in particular.

Talking about class diversity is a common way that longtime residents of Southeast talk about their history in the neighborhood. Tana talks about where she lived growing up in Anacostia: "My father was an engineer, and my mother was a homemaker. And my father was an engineer coming out of college, as a mathematician. And we lived right next door to a lady who was a hairdresser, and her husband was a home inspector. So people had careers. You know, they had careers."

In chapter 1 I argue that most discussions of gentrification erase the existence of the Black middle class, which has a profound effect on Anacostians' ability to frame gentrification as a racial process. Emphasizing the existence of the Black middle class, conversely, serves the purpose of reinforcing the idea that Anacostia specifically, and the Southeast Quadrant more generally, is a location where socioeconomic class diversity has always been in place.

Anacostia residents counter outsiders' framing that emphasizes poverty and violence by reframing their neighborhood as a place with a thriving, stable middle class and where African American people do not live in poverty but rather are part of a collaborative family and community structure that enables them to thrive. This reframing fits with the overarching characterization of a prosperous Washington, DC, and builds on the history of the District as a place where African Americans found success and opportunity.

With the notable exception of Frederick Douglass, DC's Black elite mostly settled west of the Anacostia River, favoring neighborhoods such as LeDroit Park, Upper Sixteenth Street, and Georgetown in the Northwest Quadrant. These elites sent their children to the District's private schools, several of which began welcoming wealthy Black students in the 1940s, most notably Georgetown Day School and Sidwell Friends (the latter being the prep school in the Tenleytown neighborhood that the daughters of Presidents Clinton and Obama attended). By contrast, even within the Black community the neighborhoods east of the river did not necessarily have a reputation for Black affluence. However, the fact that a population of at least middle-income, if not affluent, Black residents make their home in Anacostia is a continually evoked theme among those who hold stake in the neighborhood's culture and future. "One misconception I think people have about Anacostia is that it's not diverse," ANC member Tracey tells me. "Historic Anacostia is very diverse. It's diverse in wealth. It's diverse in class. Not as diverse in race, but there is diversity there that I d– I don't think a lot of people know about because people just don't know."

Anacostians emphasize class diversity as a means of countering the narratives about poverty in the area. While census statistics support the belief that there are significant differences in income and wealth between the two sides of the Anacostia River, it is also the case that multigenerational Washingtonians living East of the River are families who came to Anacostia because of its beauty and its Black community. They have established themselves over the years, a fact which does not go unnoticed when people migrate in and out of the neighborhood. Tracey says,

> If you attend ANC meetings you see [the old money]. You see the, um, uh younger transplants—Black couples or individuals who've moved into the Anacostia, the Congress Heights, the Bellevues. I mean every Ward 8 community . . . I mean one of our meetings– it was on the news and you saw it. There was literally a divide between, um, established African Americans and African Americans who are not so established . . . And I was like, wow. Like, that's what people don't realize. Like some of the arguing is literally between the new and the old here. It's fascinating.

Tana, when asked if there are noticeable differences between Anacostia, where she grew up, and the neighboring community of Congress Heights, less than a mile away, similarly offers, "Yeah I think that some people, especially people who have lived in Congress Heights for a long time, people who have lived there for thirty years or more, think they see themselves as you know, slightly higher brow but eh, I think that's just part of the stratification that goes on among Black people."

This emphasis on stratification serves to underscore the idea, for both women, that Southeast communities have always included affluent African Americans. This is important not only for countering inaccurate opinions about Anacostia's impoverishment but also for countering ideas of how Anacostia is changing and who gets to change it. Most people understand gentrification as a process whereby people of more affluence move into a place where a less-affluent population already lives; as geographer and urban planner Jason Hackworth puts it, gentrification is "the production of urban space for progressively more affluent users."[11] Recognizing a given process as being gentrification, therefore, assumes that the space being gentrified belongs to people who are not already affluent. By emphasizing that socioeconomic class diversity has always been present in the neighborhood, residents are both countering the narratives of Anacostia as being impoverished and combating the notion that their neighborhood should gentrify— they are declaring it is not an area with lower-income people.

The rejection of forced-positioning results in Insider Discourses that reframe the neighborhood: instead of being urban and dirty, it is rural and bucolic; instead of being crime-ridden and dangerous, it is close-knit and safe; and instead of being impoverished and in need of gentrification, it is home to middle-class residents who can take care of their own. These Insider Discourses also serve a second important function: they re-create the neighborhood as desirable, which in turn allows residents to argue against the ways that others might try to take their neighborhood away.

### "You're Offered Something Here": Counterpositioning to Emphasize Commodification

"I don't know if they thought we was going to eat 'em, or what," says Amy, Tana's ninety-three-year-old godmother, who raised her children and grandchildren in Anacostia before retiring to her daughter's home in Northwest. "[White people] used to be scared to come into Anacostia. But now that they– they don't want that long commute– Virginia, far out in Maryland– now they want to live and take over space, and they don't mind taking over space where Black people used to live."

The residents' reframing highlights the hidden aspects of the neighborhood—its amazing vistas, the foxes and deer that roam where chickens once did—as reasons anyone should want to be in Anacostia, reasons of which other Washingtonians are unaware. But as the neighborhood grows into the twenty-first century, increasingly both city officials and other residents have recognized that Anacostia is an appealing place to live. As Anacostia residents grapple with this change, the very reasons they cite for living in their neighborhood become the reasons that others want to come into it.

After describing Anacostia's bucolic beauty, Gus immediately reframes his discussion of the features of Anacostia that make it small, welcoming, and friendly as precisely the reasons that the neighborhood is being encroached upon:

> I mean, if you look at the demographics now, I mean seriously,
> you- you- you- you see more and you see more whites in the
> neighborhood now. Because it offers something here. You're
> offered– you're offered peace and quiet. Schools. Neighborhoods.
> You know, it's– it's nice. And then if you leave here, if you leave
> here and go out there to, and I say this, out to Ward 9? Which is
> PG County. You know it's going be hard getting back in here.

In Gus's description the beauty of Anacostia is both the reason current residents want to live here and a commodity that will be taken. Many explanations of gentrification are rooted in under-standings of the ways in which space itself becomes commodified: the stores, homes, and streetscapes of a community slowly change in ways designed to appeal to people with a different sense of what their space should look like.[12]

Besides the beauty and the "peace and quiet," many Anacostians cite the sense of removedness from the city without the loss of access as a principal reason people want to come. As Amy says, "They don't want that long commute." For Amy and Gus, the en-croachment of others into Anacostia is all about some people be-ing moved out and excluded as new people move in.

Through the metaphorical extension of smallness to closeness, the contrasting of a once-close community to its present-day dis-tance, and the placement of emphasis on beauty and ruralness, Anacostians' framing implicitly instantiates their experience as one through which outsiders' mistaken opinions of the neighbor-hood contribute to making Anacostia a hidden gem.

The problem with hidden gems, of course, is that once they are no longer hidden, everyone wants them. Particularly for the middle-class residents of Anacostia, this influx of new people who want the space turns the neighborhood into a less-desirable place. To critique these newcomers, however, requires a very careful bal-ance of not overtly criticizing the neighborhood but still being able to acknowledge that the neighborhood undergoing its current change is less than it once was. The ways this happens are subtle: residents use the same rejections of Outsider Discourses about the neighborhood to criticize change.

## Stancetaking and Covert Critique

Many interviewees mentioned the neighborhood's closeness and small physical boundaries; others emphasized how it has changed over time, for instance, in the ways that residents behave toward one another. These discourses play out differently depending on who is employing them. They also reflect the varying claims interviewees make to the place of Anacostia and illustrate the stances they take about the neighborhood and the ways it is changing.

Two additional concepts are also crucial in understanding how residents give meaning to the space of Anacostia: the affective and epistemic stances described earlier. Looking at the epistemic and affective stances the interviewees take in this study helps explain the nature of the residents' relationships with their community. The ways that they compare present to past allow them to take epistemic stances that privilege them as authorities on the neighborhood; taking affective stances allows them to criticize the neighborhood while still condemning outsiders whose criticisms of the neighborhood are seen as an attack.

A prime example comes from Justin, the theater teacher at the local elementary school, when he talks about the ways that the community looked out for one another:

> You don't see children outside playing anymore. You don't see
> that. You see, um, you have to have, um, organized activities if
> that's– places that you go to. And you- you- you hardly see that,
> that kind of thing so. You know Halloween? Because you knew
> your neighbors, and you– you could go around, you know, the
> block and knock on doors. The expectation that, um, every adults
> were responsible for every child within their view. The idea that
> you were safe as a child, because if someone was bothering you,
> all you had to do is go and stand by an adult. And you– you had
> that sense of safety, the sense of knowing people. And even if you
> did not know that adult, that sense that– you knew that that adult
> be– by virtue of the fact there was an adult, was cared about you
> and your safety. There was a sense of understanding what your
> boundaries were. So that's one of the– the biggest things. Speak
> ing to people. Always saying hi. You know the expectation when
> you walk down the street, you pass another human being, you're
> gonna say "Hello," you're gonna say "Good morning," you're gonna

say something. So, um, that– that sense of, of neighborhood has been missing.

When asked about how Anacostia has changed over the years, Justin points immediately to the ways in which people looked out for one another in the past. At first this sounds exactly like the strategies that others use to reject the idea that the neighborhood lacks cohesion. However, Justin uses the rejection of the forced-positioning of his neighborhood to contrast the former close-knittedness of the neighborhood with its current state, but without coming out and saying that he thinks the neighborhood has changed in a negative way. It allows him to keep from having to overtly articulate a position about the negative changes. But the affective stance-taking is still present in the way he contrasts old versus new, then versus now. Justin is able to suggest—without really saying it—that the past was different than the present. Now, according to Justin, one can't go around the block, or expect that adults will be responsible, or expect that children and adults alike will greet each other and create a sense of safety. He uses the ideal image of a place where children play outside and adults look after them to construct a negative stance toward what the neighborhood is becoming. He contrasts what "you" could do in the past and what "you" can do in the present, positioning himself in opposition to what "you" can currently see.

In fact, Justin's use of *you* is even more complicated. *You* is the subject of nearly every clause in this excerpt. However, there are two different "yous" being used in this segment. One is the you that is a somewhat generic "one" who invites the interviewer to put herself in the shoes of a person currently evaluating the neighborhood; this is the you who "[doesn't] see children playing anymore." I will call this $you_1$ Another you has the referent of Justin from the time when the neighborhood met the ideal against which he contrasts its current state: "you were safe as a child" could easily be "I was safe as a child." The second-person nature of both these referents invites the listener to place herself in the shoes of Justin-who-was and Justin-who-is, implicitly asking the listener to consider how the neighborhood has changed, as though it is part of her own experience. I call this second person, the inviting *you*, you₂.

In his discussion of change, Justin contrasts the neighborhood as it once was through his parallel syntactic structure of *you* [verb] coupled with the changing referents of *you*. To explore this in more depth, I present the excerpt in intonation units, which are the units of talk which a speaker uses to organize his or her own speech; these units are usually marked by a prolonged pause in the speech or an intake of breath.[13] (For this reason they are also called "breath groups.") For instance, a sentence with a single clause might be one intonation unit: *I threw the ball*. But a sentence such as "First my teacher gave us a warning, then we went outside, and even though my friends told me not to, I threw the ball" has four units: *First my teacher gave us a warning | then we went outside | even though my friends told me not to | I threw the ball*. In lines 1–5 Justin begins with the things that "you don't see":

1. you₁ don't see children outside playing anymore
2. you₁ don't see that
3. you₁ see um
4. uh you₁ have to have um organized activities if that's– places that you go to
5. and you₁, you₁, you₁ hardly see that, that kind of thing so

Through the repetitive structure Justin builds a case for what's missing: children playing beyond the structure of the organized activities that dominate children's schedules in the 2010s. His syntactic structure has the effect of highlighting the "don't/don't/ hardly" (lines 1, 2, and 5, as contrasted with lines 3–4) and thus quickly establishes that there is a negative change going on in the neighborhood. Justin uses the same pattern when he shifts to the "you" whose referent is "me/my peers as a child":

8. and you$_2$, you$_2$ could go around, you know the block
9. and knock on doors um
10. the expectation that um
11. every uh
12. uh adults were responsible for every child within their view
13. the idea that you$_2$ were safe as a child
14. because if someone was bothering you$_2$
15. all you$_2$ had to do is go and stand by an adult
16. and you$_2$, you had that sense of safety, the sense of, of knowing people
17. and even if you$_2$ did not know that adult, that sense that
18. you$_2$ knew that that adult be– by virtue of the fact there was an adult was cared about you$_2$ and your$_2$ safety

Interestingly, this pattern directly contradicts the pattern of the first structure, in that none of these statements contains negation. The present-tense you$_1$ in the first section is reiterated three times as "you don't / hardly see," but the past-tense you$_2$ in the second has no negation: "you$_2$ could go around" (line 8), "you$_2$ were safe" (13), "you$_2$ had that sense of safety" (16), and "you$_2$ knew that that adult" (18). In fact, the only spot where *you* is the safe child of the past or the sentence has any sort of negation is in line 17: "even if you did not know that adult." The negation is inside an embedded clause whose main purpose is to set up the contrast in line 18: "you knew that adult." Together the past versus the present *you* and the presence and the absence of negation create a contrast between the neighborhood that was and the neighborhood that is.

All of this back-and-forth between you$_1$ and you$_2$, coupled with the negation, contributes to Justin's ability to take the stance that the overall change in the neighborhood has not been positive but without having to explicitly say so. The contrast is created entirely through syntactic structure in the reiterations of what "you don't see" and in the shifting referent of *you*. This allows Justin to critique the neighborhood in which he's lived his whole life without explicitly criticizing any specific aspect that it has lost; he remains positive with the things he says about his neighborhood even as he takes up a negative stance toward how it has changed.

Tana, another middle-class Anacostian, uses a nearly identical strategy of contrasting to take up a negative affective stance regarding the neighborhood. When asked about how the neighborhood has changed, she, like Justin, offers a description emphasizing the safety and friendliness of the neighborhood. She focuses on Barry Farm, where she and her brother attended preschool, a part of the neighborhood that is an especial target of Discourses of poverty and crime. She both rejects that outsider positioning of Barry Farm by invoking the Insider Discourse of safety, then goes further to use that Insider Discourse to contrast the past with the present, creating the same negative stance toward change:

> We never felt unsafe there. Didn't feel unsafe. There were playgrounds there. The swimming pool was there. There was a basketball court. A baseball diamond. A smaller pool that we called "the Bathtub." So but that community started to really change, I think in the late seventies, you know as people began to move out. Some people began to move out. The seams seem to be fraying, or something. You know, where you didn't know as many people there as you knew before, or people didn't speak to you as much as they did before.

Like Justin, Tana draws an immediate contrast between what was and what is, through the use of words like "didn't feel unsafe." Although she does not specifically claim that currently she feels unsafe (or she would if she were to visit Barry Farms), her use of *didn't* contrasts with an unstated difference: because in the past she did not feel unsafe automatically creates an implicature that at the moment she or others do feel unsafe. This contrast allows her to evaluate negatively the change that has taken place in her neighborhood and present it as a change away from an ideal but without specifically stating so.

Tana talks about the change in terms of a dwindling of interpersonal relationships. Just as Justin says, "You know the expectation when you walk down the street, you pass another human being, you're gonna say 'Hello,' you're gonna say 'Good morning,' you're gonna say something," Tana echoes the same sentiment in her own words: "You know, where you didn't know as many people there as you knew before, or people didn't speak to you as much as they did before." Thus for both Tana and Justin one of the key things that is missing is the "sense of neighborhood" and the interactions that neighbors have with each other.

This contrasting of past to present serves an especially important purpose for middle-class residents. As I argue later, middle-class residents are poised to benefit from investments in the community more than their neighbors will; they are the ones who have the ability to spend at new restaurants and coffee shops and who won't need to leave the Southeast Quadrant for shopping opportunities (see chapter 4). However, to overtly support these things might be seen as support for the negatives of gentrification, particularly the displacement of their neighbors. By contrasting past and present, speakers can provide a covert critique which leaves space for the interpretation that there is room for improvement even while rejecting the same Outsider Discourses and invoking the same Insider Discourses in the midst of the critique.

Not all middle-class critiques of the neighborhood are so covert. Jackie, the school administrator, is another middle-class Anacostian. In the following excerpt she discusses the lack of work ethic she sees among some young people in the Anacostia neighborhood, including the parents of many students at her school. She makes a remarkably similar use of a $you_2$ to critique the increase in the joblessness rate in the neighborhood:

I have to get up every day and go to work, so $you_2$ should have to get up every day and go to work and not depend on the government, to take care of $you_2$. I could see it for the elderly; the elderly

elderly that has put in their time. You know they work. They've done all they could do. I could see them getting support from the government. But when you$_2$ young, you$_2$ in your$_2$ twenties and you$_2$ don't wanna work? Something's wrong with you$_2$. Something is really wrong. And I just don't mean to be hard or anything but, something is really wrong. So . . . I really don't know. You$_1$ know when I was coming up, this used to be a, um, heavy drug area. That avenue, so when you$_2$ in that mode and you$_2$ just wanna . . . sit there and get easy money, you$_2$ not gonna make it out here. 'Cause it's either gonna be death or penitentiary.

Jackie's use of a non-co-present *you* (similarly marked as you$_2$) allows her to critique the changes in the neighborhood that she finds undesirable, just like Justin does. But Jackie's critique is more overt than Justin's: she expresses a distinctly negative affective stance in "Something's wrong with you$_2$." At the same time, the use of the general *you* allows Jackie to critique what she sees as a process rather than criticizing any one particular group.

Jackie's talk adds one additional layer of subtle language use: the zero copula. In AAL grammar, the copula verb *be* is optionally expressed: the grammar permits both "when you're young" and "when you young." Jackie uses the absent copula to delineate the you$_2$: with each instance of *you [are]*, where *you* is this imaginary addressee of the assistance-getter, the copula is unexpressed:

when you$_2$ Ø young
you$_2$ Ø in your$_2$ twenties

This absence, though very subtle, serves to further separate this you$_2$. Jackie's use of the generic *you* allows her to distance herself and take up a stance criticizing those who rely on government assistance for what she evaluates as laziness by comparing them to the "elderly elderly," who she sees as deserving of their money.[14] In addition, the zero copula helps Jackie linguistically draw a line between the you who is co-present and the generic *you* from whom she distances herself. In this instance a subtle linguistic distinction contributes to larger patterns of stance-taking by contrast, a pattern discussed in greater detail in the next chapter.

## Conclusion

Ryane Nickens's profile in *Politico* tells a narrative that is about much more than her tremendous work in creating a new nonprofit. Even in a story ostensibly about triumph and an exploration of "good news," triumph cannot exist without first invoking the Big-D Outsider Discourses of crime, poverty, and undesirability, cementing in the minds of others the idea that Anacostia and its surrounds are, even if perhaps redeemable, largely not worthy of attention. Because advocates often frame gentrification as a boon to the people who live in the location being gentrified—new stores! new parks! cleanliness!—the circulation of Insider Discourses that claim that the neighborhood is already beautiful, safe, and wealthy implicitly counter the assumed positives of gentrification. They enable residents to stake a claim on the space and reject the notion that change is uniformly positive. The Insider Discourses give residents ways to both counter negative talk about their community and negatively evaluate the ways that it is changing.

At the same time, however, not all residents reject all Outsider Discourses. This is particularly true among middle-class Anacostians. One such final example comes from Chris, the systems analyst in his midthirties who grew up in Anacostia but later moved across the DC line into Prince George's County:

So right now right now I live in Fort Washington so that's what he was also talking about.[15] People they'll come in and then, um, people leave. People leave because, I mean, like you said there's plusses and minuses. And sometimes you know people might say the minuses outweigh the plusses, but I mean like you said it's changing. It's changing. And then probably like later, I'll probably be like, "Hey I want to get back in" and you know I'll be shut out.

Chris, who explains elsewhere in his interview that he moved over to PG County in part for his family (he had a five-month-old son at the time of the interview), says he also chose to stay in Anacostia as a young adult because of the neighborliness and community feel. In his talk he constantly surfaces both the "plusses and minus" of living in the neighborhood, then finally lands on the issue that he and his family, having chosen to leave, will likely be priced out of ever moving back.

The friction between Outsider and Insider Discourses, therefore, serves as a crucial backdrop against which nonresidents and residents view any change happening in Anacostia. On the one hand, new amenities and investment in the neighborhood mean changing the ways that nonresidents view the neighborhood—making outsider opinions match the ideas of safety, beauty, and community that residents espouse. On the other, acknowledging a need for change means accepting the forced-positioning of these Outsider Discourses to some degree. This results in the kinds of stance-taking by residents, who take up negative stances about the current state of the neighborhood through subtler strategies like contrasting old and new and referring to an abstract *you*, which permits the speaker to covertly critique aspects of the neighborhood they find less desirable without overtly using an Outsider Discourse themselves.

These covert critiques take a second form as well, as seen in the short excerpt from Jackie. The use of African American Language features in itself can be a form of covert critique and repositioning. The next chapter looks at the role that AAL plays in residents' rejection of Outsider Discourses and in the creation of a distinctly Black insider identity.

## Notes

1. Joanne Kenen, "D.C.'s Silent Gun Slaughter," *Politico*, 2018.
2. Norman McCarthy, "Does Anyone Really Care about Anacostia?,"

*Washington Post*, February 9, 1967; "Preserving Anacostia," letter to the editor, *Washington Post*, November 28, 1977.

3. Don Terry and Karen de Witt, "Toll Is Even Greater in Forgotten AnaA costia," *New York Times*, July 26, 1996; R. H. Melton, "Seeking a Greater Voice," *Washington Post*, September 6, 1960; Dana Hedgpeth, "Metro Searches for Long-Term Fix, Considers Possible Shutdown of Red Line for Water Problems," *Washington Post*, September 4, 2013.

4. Fred Reed, "A Night in Anacostia's Loose and Friendly Streets," *Washington Post*, October 5, 1992.

5. Fairclough, *Discourse and Social Change.*

6. Gee, *Social Linguistics and Literacies.* See also Gee, *Introduction to Discourse Analysis.*

7. Harré and Moghaddam, *Self and Others*, 2–3.

8. Lee, "Discourse on Southeast's Bad Reputation." Lee explores how individuals within Southeast DC use self-positioning and forced self-positioning to situate themselves and respond to outsider views of the neighborhood. I extend that work here by connecting it to the larger Discourses this positioning creates.

9. This other-positioning is not unique to Washingtonians. In a 2013 post about foreign travel advisories to Washington, the *Washington Post*'s blog GovBeat revealed that the foreign ministry of France issued a travel advisory for DC that indicated that *"Le quartier Anacostia n'est pas recommandable de jour comme de nuit"* (Don't go to Anacostia, day or night). Reid Wilson, "16 American Cities Foreign Governments Warn Their Citizens About," *Washington Post*, November 14, 2013.

10. Dale, *Village That Shaped Us*, ix.

11. Hackworth and Smith, "Changing State," 815.

12. Trinch and Snadjr, "What the Signs Say."

13. See Chafe, *Discourse, Consciousness, and Time.*

14. Her repetition of the word *elderly* in describing who should be able to receive assistance—not just "the elderly," which presumably might encompass young retirees not much older than herself, but "the elderly elderly"—is a second piece of evidence that Jackie is concerned about the ability to work.

15. Chris was jointly interviewed with Gus; excerpts of the interview apw pear in chaps. 2 and 3.

# Chapter 3

# "They Ain't Make Improvements for Us"

Place-Making with African American Language

## "Ordering the Chaos": Black Language, Black Space

In 2009, just ten days after he was inaugurated, President Barack Obama made his first visit to Ben's Chili Bowl, an icon of Washingtonian Black culture that has existed on U Street NW since 1958. Having withstood the 1968 riots and a 2010 expansion into the recently built Nationals baseball stadium, Ben's stands as an example of a Black-owned business that has "made it" and continues to do so in the District.

The president walked in, ordered a few dishes, cracked a few jokes with the workers behind the counter, and then, when it was time to pay, handed over a $100 bill. When the stunned worker tried to hand him back what was no doubt a significant amount of change, the president waved his hand and said, distractedly, "Nah, we straight."

Linguists Geneva Smitherman and H. Samy Alim say this interaction, and the media's reaction to it, worked like a magnifying glass in refracting white America's reaction to Obama's unabashed Blackness. Obama, one of the more skilled orators in the modern day, draws heavily on both white American English styles and Black American styles, particularly Black preacher style, in connecting with his audience.[1] He is as at home in the trash-talking mode of *signifyin'* or subtly putting down other speakers using shared understanding of covert meaning as he is in the soaring oratory of a State of the Union Address.[2] In a three-word utterance Obama demonstrated to the Ben's employees and the world his connection to his Blackness.

Significant, too, is not only what Obama said but *where* he said it. Ben's is right down the street from where Stokely Carmichael whipped DC's Black community into a frenzy on that night in early April 1968, a block and a half from the iconic Howard Theatre and a stone's throw from Howard University. It has withstood the effects of gentrification: as trendy new restaurants and bars, expensive condominiums, and a Whole Foods have slowly encroached on the U Street Corridor, Ben's has remained unmoved from its prime location almost directly across from the entrance to the metro.[3] It is a prime example of a Black *place:* a physical location which has been imbued with the meaning of safety and welcome for the Black community.[4] The president's use of African American Language is a three-word verification of the president's bona fides: he is a Black man, in a place for Black people, in Chocolate City.

That speech and language are connected to ideas about what it means to be a Black American is as incontrovertible for the nonspecialist listener as it is generally uninterrogated. Obama's three-word phrase is readily socially interpretable precisely because we so easily recognize this connection. And speakers exploit this connection all the time. As it is for Obama, language is a primary way in which the people of Anacostia—like people everywhere—inject meaning into their world: how they say who they are and how they want to be understood. AAL comprises various types of language practices distinct from white language practices at every level: at the phonological and morphosyntactic levels, as with the Obama example; at the intonation level; and at the discourse and rhetoric level, as it does in the practices of markin' and signifyin'— the means of teasing and putting down that some Black people use to signal in-group status and promote closeness—or in Black preacher style (which Obama also very often deployed during his presidency), where repetition of phrases and intonation evoke the style of African American preachers in African American churches.[5] As Smitherman put it in *Word from the Mother,* AAL is "a tool for ordering the chaos of human experience," in particular Black human experience.[6] AAL becomes the means by which Black Americans assert an identity which is uniquely nonwhite, occasionally oppositionally so, and which connects them to their fellow Black Americans and to the Black American experience.

Anacostia residents use various discourse strategies—framing, deixis, and Insider Discourses—to create a Black place and a unified Black community separate from gentrifying white encroachers, while along the way challenging interpretations of the neighborhood that align its Blackness with filth, crime, and undesirability. Given these broader patterns in Black discourse, it is unsurprising, then, that the same racialization processes also operate at lower levels of linguistic structure. Not only do Anacostians create particular Discourses, take up particular stances, and invoke particular frames, they also use a particular language when they do so. As it is for Obama, Black Language is an important way that Anacostians stake their claims on their Black space.

### "Whether We Was Here or Up Georgetown": Black Language Form and Function

Understanding this claim-staking requires us to take a broad look at how Anacostians understand their language use. Tana described the ways in which she and her brother noticed the new white residents of Anacostia and stood in opposition to the ways others characterized her community as something about which to be concerned. The daughter of a teacher and an engineer who was at the time of our interview completing her master's degree at Catholic University of America, she has spent her adult life working for nongovernmental organizations (NGOs) and nonprofits, and she volunteers part-time with the Community Museum. With her professional work and higher education level she seems completely different than Grey, an instructional aide in his midfifties who has a high school education, has worked the majority of his life in service industries, and is the child of parents who also were high school–educated and had similar service-oriented careers. His work and his life have been spent primarily within Southeast. Both Tana and Grey have deep roots in Anacostia, with family members having lived there for several generations.

The way Tana and Grey talk about the neighborhood is similar. Like many members of multigenerational families of Anacostians, they highlight the neighborhood's peace and its friendliness. But the *way* Tana and Grey talk about the neighborhood is different because their *metalinguistic awareness*, that is, their awareness of the linguistic structure of the language they use, their choices in using differently structured language, and their reasons for doing so, are vastly different.

Regarding most of the responses recorded in this book, at some point, typically toward the end of an interview, I would ask a question along these lines: "Tell me about what you think about language. Where do people speak differently? Does DC have a unique sound? How do you think you sound, with respect to how DC sounds?" The questions were deliberately ambiguous, inviting comment on whatever they saw as most fitting. Grey's answer focuses heavily on the communicative aspect of the language he uses:

> I don't know you asked me the same question whether we was, you know, sitting right here or up Georgetown law school, and at Barry Farm project. We can have the same conversation. So it wouldn't have made the difference. Yeah, you got to keep it real. If you don't know– the biggest mystery is for– to figure out the ins and out of person mind. And the only way you can have some clarity is if I tell you my mind, because if you try to figure it out

on your own, you would never be right. But if I tell you, and I talk to you what's in my heart, what's in my mind, that's the only way you will ever know me. Because it's— if you try to assume about you know where I live in, how much money I get, how I dress or anything else, you'll be wrong ninety-nine percent of the time. But if you hear it out my mouth you can just take it and . . . then you'll know.

Grey's focus is on the content of his speech and on the ways that talk functions as a means of interpersonal connection. For Grey, talking is about understanding and being understood; it's how "you know the ins and out of [a] person mind" and "what's in [their] heart." The focus of talk, therefore, is to uncover this mind and to understand others for who they are.

Tana, in contrast to Grey, responds to this question by focusing on her experiences getting to junior high school by crossing the river into the wealthier, more racially mixed neighborhood of Capitol Hill. In her answers she revealed a very high level of awareness of the social importance of the *form* of language, not merely its content. She begins with naming specific stigmatized forms (*ain't,* slang) and explains how her relatives provided explicit injunctions against those forms as they told her what kind of language to use:

Right, right. You know [people say], "This is not proper English, that is proper English. Don't say 'ain't.'" You know, so, um, I think that there there is a difference. But I don't know exactly what the— what makes the difference. I know that my parents did not allow us to speak a lot of slang. My brother and I would have to shift gears when it was time to go outdoors and play with our friends. So the conversations were very different. The words we used were very different. We couldn't use slang in the house but we could use it outside with our friends. But we had to— we were switching. You know, we were switching. And the language that we used at school with our friends at school was different than the language we used at home. You know, so you want to fit in at school, you want to fit in at home. So I don't think our personalities changed, but the language changed, drastically.

The way Tana's relatives taught her to speak makes her very conscious of the places and times where she uses different language, and this is evident in the way she talks about those differences. Particularly interesting is that when asked to provide an example, Tana focuses on *ain't* as an example of the words that her mother and others specifically told her not to use. Because it is a word, rather than, say, a phonological (sound) feature, the reference is highly accessible. It is very easy, for example, to tell a child "Don't say ain't" or, perhaps more troubling, that "ain't is not a word." Whereas middle-class African American families like Tana's often employ a number of features of AAL themselves, lexical items such as *ain't* provide a lightning rod of sorts on which to focus specific critique of a child's use of language.[7]

In fact, both Tana's hyperawareness of her speech and Grey's downplaying of the likelihood of his shifting exhibit the effects of what April Baker-Bell identifies as *anti-Black linguistic racism*, the "linguistic violence, persecution, dehumanization and marginalization that Black Language speakers experience in schools and everyday life" and which permeates the entire existence of Black speakers in the US context.[8] Linked to the system of racism in the United States and to hegemonically white notions which posit white speakers as a neutral norm rather than a group wielding racialized power, anti-Black linguistic racism holds that the negative ideologies that African American people internalize about language patterns that are culturally Black are a reflection of the pervasiveness of anti-Black racism more broadly.[9]

One does not need to be a linguist to notice that our language use day to day is not always perfectly the same. Most people have a sense that the way they talk in a formal setting such as school or work is different than how they sound with their friends playing cards. These changes might involve word choice, pronunciations, or wholesale changes to the grammar. Together these changes throughout the linguistic system, referred to as *style shifting,* reflect what linguist Penelope Eckert has called "the locus of the individual's internalization of broader social distributions of variation."[10] In other words, if Tana observes that *ain't* is a word that her friends use at school but one that her mother and father do not use at home, she might choose to use *ain't* to, as she puts it, "fit in at school," shifting to a variety that more closely matches that of her schoolmates.

There are many explanations for why people shift and what they shift between. The shift might involve words, like Tana's *ain't,* or whole varieties, like African American English or Southern English, but it might also involve subtle changes in the linguistic system at the level of phonology, such as whether *car* is pronounced "kah."[11] Over the decades linguists have sought many explanations for these shifts. In early foundational work William Labov explored the role of attention to speech on the shifting of phonology, giving his interviewees multiple ordered tasks: first, they were interviewed, then asked to read a passage that unobtrusively contained words which would condition the sound Labov was interested in, and finally asked to read a list of words which contain the sound in isolation.[12] In this way Labov constructed the interviews so that the speakers' focus was increasingly drawn toward the form of the language rather than its function. As the speaker is drawn more toward the form of the language, it becomes possible to observe the speaker's awareness of the "need" to shift it. This explanation of shifting formed the basis for much early sociolinguistic work in urban areas, including in Washington, DC.[13]

However, one problem with studying how people change their speech throughout an interview is that various changes have different meanings unto themselves. For instance, a single use of *didn't nobody tell me nothing* might mark a speaker in a particular way—as uneducated, as tough, as African American—yet the use of something like *dis* for *this* might happen variably throughout the interview and might contain some of the same meanings of toughness but be interpreted differently. This difference of interpretation is key to our understanding as listeners and is one of the key critiques of the attention-to-speech model of exploring "vernacularity." One of the chief problems with assuming that there is a continuum that stretches from careful to casual speech is the idea that a given variable will only show up in one form or the other and that its presence or absence indicates the social evaluation of that variable. As many recent studies have shown, the dichotomy is nowhere near that neat.

To give an example, consider the variation of word-final (ING), that is, the pronunciation of words like *walking* as *walkin'*, which has been linked to African American ethnoracial identity, tough male identity, and Southernness.[14] Scholars have shown that the *perception* of this variable matters—when we add back in the assumptions that a listener makes about who is speaking, what they are speaking about, and other aspects of a given situation (e.g., such as their authority to speak on a topic), we get a whole host of meanings for both the *walkin'* and the *walking* forms: it might indicate to a listener the degree of education, the degree of easygoingness, the degree of formality, or the degree of pretentiousness.[15] And at any given time a speaker might *recruit,* or purposefully use, that particular linguistic form in order to convey one of these meanings through her speech.

For many African Americans the host of language features available for recruitment is vast. African American Language, the variety I am interested in here, has arguably had more scholarly attention than any other nonstandardized variety of English. Often called Ebonics in the nonacademic sphere, AAL consists of a host of stylistic choices that many speakers use to mark themselves as part of the African American community.[16] These consist of sound features (such as vowel changes, changes in the pronunciation of consonants, and intonational changes) and lexical word features (such as using *ashy* to describe dry skin).

When Tana talks about moving back and forth between her two varieties, she isn't talking simply about what is right or wrong but about who she is. Asked to elaborate on her answer or give examples of "school" language and "home" language, she adds, "We might say *ain't* with our friends at home. We wouldn't say that with friends at school. We would say something different. We would say *aren't– are not.* Things as simple as that. Things as simple as that. And that was just– it was common."

In sending their children to school across the river, Tana's parents created a world for them that encompassed two different friend groups. Tana and her brother therefore had their friends in Anacostia who went to the schools on the east side of the river and their friends in Capitol Hill on the west side. These two different groups required different levels of linguistic accommodation, to "fit in" with the peers at home in Anacostia versus with the friends across the river.

Despite her insistence that the switching was something "you didn't think about," Tana's metalinguistic commentary reveals a high level of awareness of the need for, and usefulness of, style-shifting as she navigated the various aspects of her life. This kind of switching is deeply entrenched in African American identity, class identity, and place identity—one side of the river is the community where *ain't* is the right word to use, and the other side is where it is not.

While Tana describes her shifting as "common" and "as simple as that," it is anything but as simple as that. Her understanding that crossing the river into the whiter, more affluent Capitol Hill neighborhood for school necessitated her dropping of a highly marked African American Language feature such as *ain't* reflects a relationship with language which is anything but neutral. Her dropping of *ain't* happens in a place associated with other kinds of social prestige: education, greater wealth, and, importantly, whiteness—a racial fact which goes unexplored in her explanations of her own switching.

Grey's comment that his communication with me would be the same "whether we was sitting right here . . . [or at] Georgetown Law School or at Barry Farms" is not incorrect when taken from a standpoint of the communicative aspect of language; it is likely true that we would discuss the same sorts of topics and possibly even the case that he would discuss them to the same depth. However, it is unlikely that the language itself would not change, for all of the reasons that Tana notices: the chosen language itself does the work of helping her traverse the boundaries of school, home, and east and west of the river. So even though language is no doubt a part of "knowing a person mind," as Grey is sure, it is just as much about how one navigates the landscape of difference. Nevertheless, this, too, exhibits aspects of internalization of the racist structures conditioning speakers' switching; the rejection of the idea that switching happens or that the form of language matters suggests that a certain hegemony has been accepted, one which posits that erasure of linguistic difference is the answer.

We see further examples of this internalization of the ideas of white standardized varieties as superior in the talk of Justin, Robert, and Lucy, three other Anacostians who, like Tana, are employed in skilled professional occupations and hold advanced degrees. Justin, an elementary school science teacher, concurs with Tana. "I think none of us speak properly. I think when we write, we write properly: we look at our grammar, we correct, and we use a more formal style. But I think when we speak, we just speak what's quote-unquote proper for our communities and our families."

Robert, the community nonprofit employee introduced in the previous chapter, is another example. Like Tana he notes his moving between linguistic forms, saying, "I often code switch, uh, depending on who my audience is and who I'm with. You know I might speak, or not use certain words when I'm in a professional environment, as opposed to, you know, a environment where it's just family and friends." Similarly, Lucy the schoolteacher offers,

> And you know, it's like, when you come to the marketplace, let's all speak, you know, that standard. So that we can get this done, you know. But when you are socializing, or you're in your– your communities, relax . . . I speak differently when I'm speaking to the parents [at the school], I speak differently when I'm speaking to kids, I speak different when I'm in a interview– job interview– or when I'm around my friends as opposed to coworkers. You know.

Like Justin, both Robert and Lucy acknowledge the inevitability of style-shifting, They link it, as many do, to audience, which linguists have argued to be one of the biggest drivers of style-shift. If a given person recognizes that they style-shift, they are most likely to tie the shift to the person to whom they are talking or the situation in which they find themselves. They do not often acknowledge the ways in which these interactions are embedded in racialized structures or in their own internalization of attitudes which reject the language-styling of Black speakers. Justin's use of terms like "proper" or Lucy's observation that the differences are based on the "marketplace" suggest an implicit agreement with racist linguistic ideologies which position white standardized varieties above African American Language varieties and privilege the latter in places that have social prestige, like school or work.[17] Yet in grappling with the sense that they can control these switches and make them deliberately, they engage in what Baker-Bell calls Linguistic Double Consciousness: a speaker both resists Anti-Black Linguistic Racism and its attendant perpetuation of white linguistic hegemony but also at times perpetuates it. Lucy and Tana do not interrogate what it is about the marketplace or the school which make them less likely to use AAL in particular, and they avoid commenting on the ways in which these places are racialized. Justin does take it a step further into a discussion of the ways in which AAL is the right language by redefining "proper" language to be not merely the one considered most prestigious, but rather the one most appropriate for the situation. At the same time, like Lucy and Tana, Justin does not explicitly link the idea of standardized varieties with privileged places, and he certainly does not engage with the ways the standardized varieties are racialized in the first place.

Yet AAL is deployed in style-shifting by all these speakers, whether its purpose is explicitly acknowledged or not. In the same way that not acknowledging the coupling of the use of a white standardized variety in a white space can make the act of using that white variety seem to be de-racialized, using style associated with AAL can racialize something which on the surface may seem as though it is not about race. The quantitative data I present in this chapter shows that there's more to style-shifting than just the person on the other end of the conversation; with the exception of two interviews with interviewee pairs (Lucy and Oliver, Gus and Chris) and one interview with the Anacostia seniors group, the speech that I analyze comes entirely from interviews that consist of only the unilateral interaction between interviewee and interviewer. This suggests that in fact, whether discussed overtly or not, speakers recognize and employ the linkages between racialized ways of speaking in order to emphasize their connection to a racialized place.

### Studying Shift

Ideally, if we wanted to understand the differences in Tana's speech we would follow her, as a girl, from one side of the river to the other, observing the kind of language she uses in one locale versus another. However, this kind of study is generally impractical, particularly for studying many people, as is the case in this work.[18] The Labovian interview task had interviewees step through multiple tasks during the interview, with the goal of observing how their language changes through those tasks based on the attention they are paying to the form of their language rather than its communicative function. Labov sees these tasks as separate from the portion of the interview that many would consider the most "interview-like," the portion where the interviewer asks the interviewee to talk on a range of topics so as to elicit as much naturally occurring speech as possible. That portion, however, can also be a site for exploring how individuals shift and for probing the connections that speakers are making between their language and its potential for different kinds of meaning.

From the start of the explorations of African American Language, many linguists have documented inventories of its morphosyntactic features, that is, the features that differ from the grammar and the inflectional word-formation patterns of standardized varieties of English in regular, patterned ways.[19] I use the term *standardized* to acknowledge that the definitions of "standard" varieties—those that usually correspond to the varieties of English spoken by the most societally privileged groups, who are often white, higher socioeconomic status, and male—reflect a process related to the hegemonic privilege accorded to their speakers rather than to any linguistically observable fact.[20] These grammatical differences, along with other differences in the African American Language system, have been long documented as a significant way that African American identity and often nonwhite identity are indexed through language. Studying the ways that African Americans systematically use features of AAL in style-shifts gives insights into some aspects of this identity work.

The residents of Anacostia intertwine race identity and place identity in the strategies they use to racialize gentrification and reject the discourses in circulation about their neighborhood. The same linkage process that happens in discourse is also reflected in language structure itself. Anacostians bind race and place identity together through the ways they use AAL in talking about Anacostia and Southeast generally, and particularly in talking about how Anacostia is changing.

Comparing style-shifting across speakers is complicated, in part because the rate at which any individual speaker uses features of a given language variety is bound to be different from that of another speaker. If Tana generally uses *ain't* infrequently, it might be more significant that she uses it at all when east of the river than it would be for someone else who uses it at nearly every opportunity. What is needed is a way to compare intraspeaker variation, that is, the variation that exists within a given person's talk, across speakers. We need some way of studying style-shifting in the aggregate.

One way linguists have done this is through the dialect density measure (DDM).[21] DDM takes known features of a language variety, often African American Language, and explores them in the aggregate, quantifying the rate at which they occur in the language of a given speaker. This creates what is known as a composite index: it treats all parts of the variety as equal and combines them into a single measure. Scholars have often employed DDM in studies of academic achievement among African American grade schoolers, and some have recently used it in longitudinal studies of African American Language change across the lifespan, and, importantly, as a part of style-shifting in AAL.[22]

DDM has been criticized for a number of its aspects. First, it treats all features of a variety as quantitatively equal, even though studies of AAL have long shown that specific features behave differently due to both linguistic and social factors.[23] In addition, DDM's use in grade schools has been criticized as a reductionist means of further marginalizing already marginalized children: a high-DDM student, while potentially being targeted for "intervention," has nevertheless already been *targeted* and her native variety identified as being overused to the point of academic distress.[24]

At the same time, many of the foundational studies of AAL style-shifting have found similar patterns of features at the same linguistic level: for instance, that both morphosyntactic variables and phonological variables are likely to shift in the same way. Therefore, I have chosen here to look at only one aspect of AAL style: those changes that are part of the morphosyntactic system.

A second reason for looking only at morphosyntactic features of AAL is that they are the kinds of features a person is likely to be more aware of. A speaker's awareness of the meaning attached to a particular variant can affect their conscious choices regarding its use. This awareness often does pattern along lines of social class— speakers who have higher socioeconomic status are more likely to have received specific injunctions regarding particular words and phrases and are more conscious of their use. The features that interviewees comment on most often are lexical, morphological, or syntactic—recall Tana's "we couldn't use 'ain't'" at the opening of this chapter. Speakers are much less likely to comment on phonological features of their language, and when they do, their remarks lack the specificity of their commentary about their lexical and morphosyntactic items.[25] Very often such remarks consist of comments like "younger people mumble" or ascribe patterned phonological features to "lazy pronunciation."

Morphosyntactic features are more likely to vary in styleshifting, both within a given speaker's style and between speakers. Linguists have shown that morphosyntax is more likely than phonology to vary more sharply when comparing the talk of speakers of different social classes versus the talk of a single speaker among different audiences.[26] They also find that morphosyntactic features are more likely than phonological features to be absent in the speech of middle- and upper-class African Americans.[27] We talk about these "more noticed" features as being more *marked* than features which are less-noticed. These more-marked features, therefore, have the potential to tell us a great deal about the kinds of meaning that a person assigns to a given shift—if they are more likely to be aware they are doing it and more likely to inhibit it, then its use is likely more meaningful.

In calculating the density of features, I rely on a modification of the method Craig and Washington used in counting features per unit.[28] For the purposes of this study I tagged AAL morphosyntactic features according to their instance per *intonation unit,* the building blocks of longer discourse into which speakers organize their speech.[29] I then divided the number of AAL features by the total number of intonation units within each topic to arrive at a percentage calculation of density.

The Features

Tana focuses on *ain't,* one of the most highly lexical features of AAL. As I mentioned, this one is particularly easy to teach and is often a feature of grammar corrections to younger speakers. AAL, however, is a complex linguistic system with a variety of features that result in a grammar that is different than standardized English varieties. These differences have been extensively cataloged elsewhere.

All thirty-four interviews that were conducted as part of this project were coded to this system, and the initial coding of any feature known to be part of AAL was included. If it was unclear whether a feature is an AAL feature, it was left out to reduce possible confirmation bias. For example, one possible feature of AAL is the use of the article *a* before any noun, regardless of whether that noun begins with a vowel, which in standardized varieties would usually require *an.* However, because for most speakers the article *a* sounds exactly the same as the filler word *uh,* if a given interviewee produced "a apple" but from context the speech was disfluent and the speaker seemed to be searching for a word and thus it was possible that perhaps they meant "uh . . . apple," then this instance was not coded.[30]

I also considered any AAL feature that occurred fewer than two times in a given interview as an "other" feature, but any individual feature that occurred three or more times was coded. This led to a total of thirteen morphosyntactic features of AAL, which are presented, with examples, in table 1.

One of the difficulties of doing a traditional variationist analysis of morphosyntactic variables is that variationist analyses rely on comparing potential realizations to actual realizations.[31] But for morphosyntactic variables, coding for sites of potential realizations can be complex if not outright impossible. For instance, while coding for existential *it* might seem to be a straightforward task—simply counting, at all, the locations where the speaker could say *there is,* whether the speaker says *there is* or *it is*—the full range of possibilities for existentials also includes much more complex constructions: for example, "You've got" in "You've got your red balls in this bin, and you've got your yellow balls in that bin." (And, of course, this example also includes got/have alternation.) While some features, such as zero copula, are highly patterned, or at least can definitely be said to be barred in certain constructions, other features, like existentials, are considerably more variable, so explaining whether or not a site is a potential site for that variant to occur is not a straightforward task.[32] For these reasons, potential realizations are not coded. Rather than providing a strictly variationist analysis, this approach leads to overall quantitative evidence about how AAL grammar patterns appear in discourses about place.

There are several reasons for exploring this patterning quantitatively and in the aggregate. The first is that for all speakers, even those who might be considered to use AAL features extensively, actual usage rates when measured quantitatively are fairly low. The interviewee with the highest rate of AAL use in this book, Gus, barely reaches 16 percent of intonation units containing at least one AAL morphosyntactic feature; if one could splice together the other intonation units in his interview without losing their meaning, the impression given—at least by the text, as intonation and phonology add to the effect, of course—would be that of a relatively mainstream, standardized English speaker.

## Table 1. AAL Morphosyntactic Features

| Feature | Description | Example |
|---|---|---|
| Zero copula | Direct linking of a subject and adjective subject predicate without the linking verb *to be* | He Ø nice |
| Negative concord | Negation shown by adding negation markers to multiple words in a sentence | Don't nobody want that |
| Determiner-leveling | Use of *a* for all nouns regardless of initial vowel or consonant segment, and bare nouns; a countable noun produced without the determiner* | A egg <br> Suit look good on you |
| Past-tense-leveling | Use of present tense in past temporal constructions | Yesterday she say I look good |
| Completive done | *Done* used to mark the past completion of an action | I done ate my lunch |
| Remote time (stressed) *been* | *BIN* used to mark something that has been happening for a long time and is still happening | I BIN had my supplies |
| Third singular verb regularization | Use of the same verb paradigm for all persons and numbers (no inflection on verbs) | He talk to her every day |
| Habitual *be* | Uninflected *Be* used to mark habitually occurring actions and states | We be having to write a lot in this class |
| Existential *it* | *It* used to mark existential existence (instead of *there*) | It was a lot of tourists downtown |
| *ain't* | *Ain't* | They ain't here |
| *they* substitution | *They* used as third-person plural possessive | Those girls don't have they homework |
| *got* for *have/has* | *Got* used in place of *to have* | She got four kids |
| Q-inversion | Questions in embedded clauses without the inversion of the subject and auxiliary | He asked her would she dance with him |

* See Spears, "Bare Nouns in African American English (AAE)."

Second, many linguists have found that many of the most marked features of AAL decrease significantly as the socioeconomic status of the speaker rises. Middle-class African Americans are more likely to use what linguist Arthur Spears and others have termed "Black Standard English," a language style that incorporates features of AAL that are less marked and are often phonological features, rather than things like *ain't*.[33] Their speech winds up having a distinctly African American nature even while it avoids many of the most stigmatized forms. In fact, some work shows that African American listeners prefer this Black Standard English: when asked in one study to identify appropriate-sounding speech for situations such as a student talking to a teacher or giving a formal report, most African American parents choose the BSE speaker over both the speaker who uses more marked AAL features *and* over the one who speaks a variety that is closer to the privileged white variety.[34]

Because this work concerns itself with features that are on the more marked end of the spectrum, it is necessary to look at quantitative patterning at a fairly broad level in order to see it at all. From that overall quantitative patterning, then, we develop a springboard from which to explore the reasons for it. Just what is it about the topics under consideration that drive this broader patterning?

### The Topics

In early studies, the chosen topic was mainly used as a means to get at the illusive "vernacular" as well as a way to elicit the features that those conducting the studies considered to be most important. As such, most interviews in these early studies took the form of the interviewer asking a question, such as "How did your family celebrate the holidays?" and then encouraging the interviewee to expound upon it at length.[35] Some of this early work followed on the idea of Labov's Attention to Speech model of shifting: the idea that conversational topics could at least cause the interviewee to shift into a slightly less formal style than a standard question/answer interview would produce.[36] Creating shifts in topic is central to the enterprise of conducting a sociolinguistic interview, to the point that some linguists have questioned whether an interview that does not proceed in the traditional topic-based module format can be considered a sociolinguistic interview at all.[37] Because the purpose of topic is understood generally as a means of facilitating data collection in the classic sociolinguistic interview, it has rarely been the object of study when it comes to style-shifting, with most studies using it, if they use it at all, to make post hoc decisions about what kinds of speech styles a particular interviewee happens to be using. Linguists have noted that topic itself and the reasons that drive topic-based shift are particularly difficult to pin down. Douglas Biber, for one, points out that "in particular, the parameter of topic needs further analysis and is perhaps not specifiable as a closed set." Alan Bell, in his conceptualization of *referee design*, argues that a shift in topic actually represents a shift in the imagined audience and that it is the speakers' desires to move toward or away from the linguistic practices of that imagined audience which drives their style shift.[38] Even the most famous study of topic shift is organized around shifts in audience rather than on shifts in topic, even though other linguists argue that topic is actually the most obvious driver for the results the authors observed.[39]

Contrary to this focus on topic simply as a means of generating data, however, are the handful of studies on topic-based shift which reveal that topic itself is a driver of stylistic shift. Robert Podesva, for instance, also working with attitudes toward gentrifying neighborhoods in Washington, DC, finds that shifts in AAL phonology effectively serve as a proxy for opposition to gentrification in the neighborhood, much as I argue that AAL morphosyntax functions here. In my own work I have found that topic can explain phonological as well as morphosyntactic shifts in Black speech styles in ways that are remarkably congruent across time and populations.[40] For instance, I have found topic to be a driver in the use of an AAL phonological feature, TH-fronting, or the pronunciation of words like *this* as *dis*: as neighbors in the same community talk about different topics, this feature varies as a way of emphasizing or deemphasizing the racialization of their neighborhood. Language variation between topics, therefore, can help explain the ways that speakers use a particular language variety to draw connections between the identities associated with that variety (in this case, AAL) and the things they are talking about.

If AAL morphosyntax is difficult to delimit, topic is even more complicated. When do we decide that a speaker has changed topic? Do only the topics of the interviewer's choosing count? What do we do if the speaker goes "off script," especially since this is exactly what we want them to do? The standard sociolinguistic interview format uses topic as a means of driving at whatever a speaker might do when they aren't being observed, and using similar topics makes data comparable across interviews. Datasets such as Ralph Fasold's from the late 1960s in Washington, DC, contain many delightfully neat interviews—first the participants talk about games they played as a child, then about school, then about Christmas, and so on. These provide nicely organized datasets for topic analysis.[41]

Yet if one of the main goals of the sociolinguistic interview is to minimize the effect of the interview setting itself, then interviews during which the speaker takes the proverbial ball and runs with it are exactly the prize we want. Among the Anacostia community members who gave me the gift of their time are many for whom the interview began with the interviewee saying something to the effect of, "I don't have very much to tell you," only to finish the interview two or three hours later.[42] Throughout that intervening time the interviewees typically went on at length about the things that most mattered to them, using my questions as a spark but ultimately taking the interview where they wanted it to go (which, of course, is exactly where I want it to go too). This leaves a jumble of information, where one speaker might talk at length about topic A and never cover topics C, D, or E. The dataset becomes quite uneven.

One complicated aspect of topic is how we define what the speaker is talking *about* anyway. In the case of a very structured interview, this is relatively straightforward: the interviewer has asked about Christmas celebrations and the lines which follow likely fall into the topic of "Christmas celebrations."[43] But what to do when "Christmas" causes the speaker to go off on a tirade about the way that schools have changed their practices for recognizing Christian holidays? Is that still "Christmas," or is it something else entirely?

One possible way to explore topic is through the lens of stance (see chapter 2). To briefly recap, stance consists of the ways that people signal their relationship toward something or someone or their relationship to what they are saying. The something, someone, or the thing that the person is saying is known as the *stance object*. Many linguists, myself included, would argue that stance-taking is at the heart of the linguistic endeavor—that the principal thing we are doing as speakers is taking stances, and that our language use must always be evaluated with respect to the stances that we are taking at any given time. It is for this reason that I believe the best way to evaluate topic is through stance: by looking at each segment of talk and identifying the stance object against which the speaker is self-positioning.

To develop a comprehensive taxonomy of topic that takes into account the tendency of a good interview to "go off the rails," I choose to investigate the stance object being evaluated in each stretch of speech. Essential to this analysis is the concept of the intonation unit, or the pitch contour into which a given talker organizes their speech. To develop the topic taxonomy I coded each intonation unit for its stance object, then I grouped smaller topics into broader or larger topic categories so as to most efficiently capture what is occurring for each speaker over a given stretch of talk. For instance, Amy talks about the Baptist church she attended in Georgetown, Delores talks about the Catholic church in Anacostia, and Chess relays his experience in a youth organization and being invited to a mosque in upper Northwest. These stance objects would begin as "Georgetown Baptist Church," "Our Lady of Perpetual Help," and "Upper NW Mosque" but eventually would be grouped into a larger topic category of "religion." This approach, informed by grounded theory, has the benefit of beginning not from the interviewer's ideas about what should or could be talked about but instead following the natural organization of speakers' talk.[44] This in turn greatly reduced the amount of bias that I as the researcher, with specific questions about place identity, neighborhood change, and race identification, can introduce into the process.

This assessment yields the following topics:

| | |
|---|---|
| Change | talk about the ways Southeast and Metro DC have changed and are changing |
| Education | talk about speaker's own education, or education in general |
| Language | talk about language, dialects, DC slang, correct language. |
| Personal history | talk about speaker's personal history, including talk about childhood activities, family |
| Race | talk about race and discrimination |
| Religion | talk about religion, church, religious experiences |
| Southeast DC | talk about Southeast Washington, DC, generally |
| Speaker-initiated | the speaker directs |
| Washington, DC | talk about the Metro DC area nonexclusive to Southeast DC |
| Work | talk about speaker's own work history, ideologies about work, gender in the workplace |

Most of the topics emerged naturally out of the conversational interview. While in general I conducted the interviews using the classic sociolinguistic module approach, whereby a series of questions on related topics was presented to the interviewee, the interview itself often meandered naturally. Most interviewees, however, talked about most of these topics, given that the interview's primary focus is on their identities as Anacostia residents. However, some interviewees talked about a topic that no other interviewees talked about, and for this reason I coded some topics as speaker-initiated. These topics are highly speaker-specific—no parallel topic can be found in another interviewee's talk.

I want to point out, however, that despite the name given to this topic type, I did not count any topic that the speaker introduced as speaker-initiated—because the interviews were about the interviewee's relationship to the community, very often other topics came up naturally before I had a chance to ask about them. For instance, a question about DC schools might lead naturally into a discussion of race if an older interviewee chose to muse on how the schools have become first more and then less integrated over time. When a given interviewee pursued a topic to the extent that it was not comparable to topics brought up by other interviewees, I code that stretch of talk as speaker-initiated.

The speaker-initiated topic is made up of two very different speech styles according to the taxonomy Labov proposed in 1972 and refined in 2012.[45] These are the "tangent" style, in which the speaker deviates plainly from the last topic the interviewer introduced, and the "soapbox" style, which is characterized by an extended expression of the speaker's opinion delivered as if to a general audience rather than directly to the interviewer. What I aim to show is that when we look for an explanation for changes in morphosyntactic features—the ones that speakers, especially middle-class speakers, are most likely to be highly aware of—the changes in the style of speech don't explain the data as well as the changes in topic do. And the fact that certain topics change more than others shows an important connection to the speakers' identities of race and place.[46]

### Density Measure Results

If we accept that style-shifting matters, we then have to determine how to best unearth whether shifting is indeed taking place. As mentioned previously, the DDM enables the establishment of an overall rate of AAL features, which can be obtained by dividing the number of intonation units having at least one AAL feature by the total number of units. Table 2 shows the breakdown of topics, with higher percentages indicating a higher rate for that topic.[47]

These results show that people do indeed change the kind of grammar they use based on what they are talking about, using far more AAL features when discussing neighborhood change than when discussing religion. In other words, a change in topic actually does change the talk the topic elicits. To put this finding in technical terms, a change in topic is a significant predictor of the presence or absence of AAL morphosyntax. Table 2 illustrates meaningful differences in the data that we can't attribute to chance.[48]

So what people are talking about matters. Looking at table 2, it's obvious that patterns exist: the topics of neighborhood change; Washington, DC; Southeast; and personal history all produce high rates. It appears, then, that while all the topics elicit some use of AAL features, some topics elicit significantly more than others— and, it turns out, these topics have important things in common.

We can quantify this difference by looking at how much any topic contributes to the overall result and by looking at the residuals of the chi-squared test or the factor weights in the regression analysis. Because the point of a chi-squared test is to pinpoint how far a distribution is from what would be expected for that population if the pattern were equal, the residuals identify which aspects

Table 2. Density Measure by Topic

|  | AAL intonation units | Total intonation units | Percentage rate |
|---|---|---|---|
| Change | 170 | 2,561 | 6.64 |
| Washington, DC | 96 | 1,682 | 5.71 |
| Race | 93 | 1,682 | 5.53 |
| Southeast DC | 155 | 3,068 | 5.05 |
| Speaker-initiated | 48 | 969 | 4.95 |
| Personal history | 157 | 3,263 | 4.81 |
| Education | 54 | 1,375 | 3.93 |
| Language | 47 | 1,319 | 3.56 |
| Gender | 26 | 778 | 3.34 |
| Work | 23 | 1,384 | 1.66 |
| Religion | 6 | 420 | 1.43 |

of the distribution are the furthest from the estimation: the larger the number, the further that particular aspect is from what would be expected. If a topic has a high residual for AAL presence, then it both significantly predicts AAL and is more predictive than topics with a lower residual. We can therefore use the residuals to obtain a rough ordering of which topics are most likely to have an AAL feature, as seen in table 3.

The chi-squared residuals for the coded topics show that race, personal history, change, and DC, in that order, exert the biggest pull on the model for having morphosyntactic features of AAL present. When talking about these topics, speakers are much more likely than average to use AAL. Conversely, the topics of work, language, religion, and education show the biggest negative impact on AAL use.

It is not surprising that talk about race predicts a higher rate of use of AAL. Both white and Black listeners expect AAL to be present when Black people talk about race, as Kate Anderson has shown.[49] Using ethnoracially marked features is part of the way in which speakers are understood to "do" race when they talk about race, and results of the large body of work on AAL more generally

Table 3. Chi-Square Residuals

| Topic | Residual |
| --- | --- |
| Work | −4.2986 |
| Religion | −2.4219 |
| Language | −1.90915 |
| Education | −1.30753 |
| Southeast DC | −1.24216 |
| Gender | −1.14863 |
| Youth | −0.44112 |
| Speaker–initiated | −0.22796 |
| Race | 1.20173 |
| Personal history | 1.942679 |
| Change | 2.766006 |
| Washinton, DC | 3.211443 |

are explicit: AAL plays a major role in demonstrating various kinds of African American identities.[50] Thus, I am not surprised that when Anacostia interviewees invoke race explicitly, they ground themselves as people who have a race; using a "raced" form of language is a major part of that. This may also explain the residual for the personal history topic: when you talk about growing up Black, *being* Black is a major part of that. In work on other data from Washingtonian speakers I have also concluded that personal history topics invite the speaker to inhabit a persona that evokes their childhood self; and in so doing they style-shift toward a more overtly African American style.[51]

What is more surprising is that the change topic and the DC topic have the strongest pull on the model, even more than race. Both of these topics cause interviewees to use more AAL morphosyntax than they do with the topic of race itself. This prompts the question: Why?

## Black Shifting

Like speakers of all ethnicities, African American speakers draw on a variety of linguistic features in everyday use—a *verbal reper-*

*toire*, to borrow linguist John Gumperz's term.[52] One of the most significant identities that a US speaker might take up is that of an ethnoracial identity. Because of the ways the US cultural context organizes race—still in many ways recognizing whiteness as the default and marking anyone who is even slightly not white as belonging to a separate group—the signaling of one's ethnoracial affiliation is a significant aspect of how any speaker, whether a person of color or white, uses their speech. Within the US African American community specifically, the relationship between language and ethnoracial identity is particularly pronounced.

Language choice, and shifting in and out of different styles, becomes deeply connected to racial identity. Speakers use language both to express and reify their racial identities, and they simultaneously attach racial ideologies and racial identities to language use, as linguists John Rickford, Arnetha Ball, and H. Samy Alim have said.[53] In short, speakers both "race language" (the latter), and use their talk to "language race" (the former). When people make connections between their language and their ethnoracial identities, they do so by drawing on existing connections that others understand and by reinforcing those meanings in their interactions. All of these features get combined into linguistic styles that are distinctively African American in nature and are used to "do" racial identity, at different times and in different ways.

This helps explain the patterning seen in the quantitative data. If language is a principal means of asserting racialized identity, then it's unsurprising to see it arise in topics closely related to race, including race itself. That we see a similar pattern with the topics of neighborhood change and DC itself suggests that these topics are similarly racialized: they, too, are places where an African American identity is at the fore.

It is particularly notable that the rate of use is high across socioeconomic statuses and that in the talk of speakers who otherwise use AAL features very rarely, their increased use becomes easy to see. For example, in talking about Washington, DC, as Chocolate

City, Robert, a middle-class interviewee who works in an organization which does planning for the neighborhood, offers this:

1. and then the different demographics change
2. um ya know
3. Washington, DC, was known as Chocolate City
4. and the reason it was known as Chocolate City
5. is because it was so
6. you know there- it [EXISTENTIAL] was so many
   African Americans
7. that lived here
8. um
9. ya know that's
10. I don't know that that can be called Chocolate City anymore
11. It's more like, you know
12. uh caramel maybe

In line 8 of this excerpt Robert uses a single instance of the existential *it*; "it was so many African Americans that lived here." This
line is set off by his searching for the right thing to say—in line 6
he makes a repair by pausing after "it was so," as he presumably
searches for the right way to phrase exactly what he is looking for.
Even more interesting is that he begins with the existential "there"
in "you know there-." This existential is the one which would be
expected for a speaker of standardized American English: consider the full sentence: "The reason it was known as Chocolate
City is because there were so many African Americans that lived
here." This is not the construction Robert uses, however, and not
only does he use the existential *it*, he in fact repairs *to* the AAL
existential pronoun. So instead of "there were so many," he stops
and produces "it was so many" instead.

Of course, this excerpt is situated within a discussion of how
Washington, DC, is changing. Robert goes on to explain that he

doesn't feel "that it can be called Chocolate City anymore," and laughs when he says it is "more like, uh, caramel maybe." Discussing how the city has changed demographically alters not only how he's describing the city but also affects his language use at the hyperlocal level. This single use of an AAL feature serves to set off the discussion of DC as Chocolate City and serves as a racialized linguistic signifier to denote that the racial component of this talk is important.

We can also return to Gus, the retired government truck driver whose talk about Anacostia's beauty and smallness featured in chapter 2. Later in his interview he addresses some of the ways that the change in the neighborhood is happening:

1. it will become bad for us
2. us meaning Black folks it's going
3. if I move out of Anacostia tomorrow
4. and want to come back
5. a house is going to cost me three times as much
6. but that's the new history of uh uh uh of Southeast
7. that's the new thing of Southeast that's going on
8. and it it there is no admittance to it.
9. Nobody wants to admit that
10. well yeah it's going on
11. no it
12. you know they'll tell you "no
13. no it's not
14. that's not happening"
15. that's a lie.
16. You can see it.
17. You can
18. You can go out there and look at the subway.
19. You can go out there and look at the bus.
20. you know come on they're doing

21. they're making vast improvements over here
22. they ain't [AIN'T] make [PROGRESSIVE LEVELING] improvements for us
23. they're not.
24. They're making improvements to get to change the demographics
25. all this history is going to be gone.

Like Delores, Gus chooses to overtly criticize the processes going on in the neighborhood. In this section of talk Gus uses several of the strategies other interviewees use to address what he sees as the threat of neighborhood change. His criticism of the change is direct and is accomplished through his use of constructed dialogue. He puts into the mouths of the people who are making the changes to the neighborhood (presumably developers and investors) the words, "No, no, that's not happening," and then follows up with his unswerving assessment of the validity of these claims. "That's a lie." He appeals to the fact that the residents of the neighborhoods can "go out there and look at the subway [and bus]" to point out that the people whose voices he is appealing to are saying something that is observably false.

Constructing the dialogue of those who insist that change is not happening allows Gus to take an epistemic stance which positions him as an expert observer. Recall from chapter 2 that an epistemic stance is how a given speaker expresses their relationship to their talk: how certain they are, what their attitude is toward the assertion itself, and not just the thing that the assertion is about. Gus gives his assertion with absolutely no hedges or any epistemic markers of uncertainty: "That's [the idea that change is not happening] a lie."

Gus also makes an important move with respect to his deictic positioning of the African American community. The strategy of using *we* to refer to the Washington African American community positions that community in opposition to white Washington and contributes to marking both Anacostia as Black space and gentri-fication and change as white phenomena. Gus uses this discourse strategy in several places: in lines 12–14 and 20–22 he refers to a "they" who are changing the community: "you know they'll tell you 'no / no it's not / that's not happening' / they're making vast improvements over here / they ain't make improvements for us."

The "they" here are the developers, in contrast to the "us" who are Anacostians. Gus in particular calls out the detrimental effects of this development by appealing to the history of Anacostia, a bastion of African American history within Washington, that am-plifies the rich African American history present in Washington as a whole. The history which "will be gone," then, is that Black history, the continued presence of the African American commu-nity which has lived here since the area was first settled. This his-tory, Gus argues, will be changed in large part because of what he understands the goal of the development to be: "to change the demographics" (line 24)—in other words, to take Anacostia from Black to white.

Given the racializing of the frame of development it should come as little surprise that at the zenith of Gus's indignation we hear him employ multiple morphosyntactic features of AAL, when he says, "they ain't [AIN'T] make [PROGRESSIVE LEVELING] improvements for us."

This exclamation uses the only two morphosyntactic features of AAL Gus used in the entire stretch of talk, and they occur next to each other: *ain't* and zero-aspect marking on *make*. This can't simply be attributed to an overall higher rate of AAL, because in the previous line Gus utters, "they're making vast improvements over here," leaving the copula verb in and fully marking *make* for the progressive aspect. Both the structure and the use of "ain't make" serve to heighten the distinction between the two sentences. Combined with Gus's "expert observer" epistemic stance-taking described earlier, his final exclamation allows him to draw a rather damning conclusion about what is happening around him.

Looking at style-shifting in the aggregate reveals a pattern that is not obvious when we look at the talk of individual interviewees. A single existential *it*, as in Robert's excerpt, is unremarkable until we realize that he, like other middle-class Anacostians, is more likely to use AAL when he is talking about issues related to place. Similarly, "they ain't make improvements for us" seems like a bold statement which just coincidentally happens to be made in the vernacular of an AAL-using speaker until it is compared with the stretch of talk before and after it. That talk about place causes the same style shifts as talk about race indicates the linkages between these two—like the strategies of stance-taking, reframing, deictic positioning, and rejection of forced-positioning explored in previous chapters, it is a way that residents use language to stake a Black claim on the place identity of Anacostia.

### Talking Race, Speaking Place

Understanding the relationship between race, language form, and identities of place helps us understand what individual speakers are doing when they make assertions about the neighborhood. It can be helpful, therefore, to trace this relationship using a single example, and for this I turn to Delores, the grandmother first introduced in chapter 1. Living on Hill Street nearly her whole life, she has watched as new neighbors have moved in and the literal landscape has changed as the city has excavated land at the top of the hill. For the most part she is excited about the changes happening to the neighborhood. "But what I think is a terrible money-wasting idea," she tells me, "is these trolley cars. They done had the tracks down for five years. I haven't seen no trolley car run yet. They have the trolley– the tracks down there by the metro, but, um, by Anacostia metro station, but the way the tro– the tracks are set up, it would be to carry people to Homeland Security."

The DC streetcar program, which began its planning process in 2002, called for streetcar tracks to be laid in two neighborhoods—

the rapidly gentrifying H Street in Northeast and along Fort Stirling Avenue in Anacostia.[54] The Fort Stirling corridor connects Joint Force Base Anacostia Bolling to the central downtown area of Anacostia, but the initial contract had the streetcar terminating at the new offices of the Department of Homeland Security without continuing into the business district. At least as initially planned the streetcar would have done a poor job of serving Historic Anacostia and mostly just connected two important government spaces to each other.

The streetcar program also became synonymous with government waste and stalled progress. The first tracks were laid on the H Street segment in 2009, seven years after the planning process had begun, and the project experienced delay upon delay, becoming a running joke in the District. While the Anacostia segment was originally predicted to open in late 2012, and the H Street segment by mid-2013, the H Street segment did not run its first trains until February 27, 2016, and as of the writing of this book, the Anacostia segment has been sidelined by the DC Department of Transportation.

Given this lack of progress, it makes sense that Delores would point to the streetcar when talking about ways the neighborhood is currently changing, and it is unsurprising that she is disappointed with the lack of progress. What is more interesting, however, is the language she uses to express this unhappiness: "They done had the tracks down for five years. I haven't seen no trolley car run yet."

In this section of the interview Delores had just informed me that because some of the DC metro system is built on the swampland of the Potomac and Anacostia Rivers, the District pays to pump millions of gallons of water out of the system every year.[55] She finds the metrorail system useful, and therefore even though this is an enormous expense to the District and its taxpayers, the benefits of having a rail system that takes people over and under the rivers is worth the expense. But then she goes on:

1. but what I think is a terrible money-wasting idea is these trolley cars
2. They done [COMPLETIVE DONE] had the tracks down for five years. I haven't seen no [NEG CONCORD] trolley car run yet
3. that was um
4. Adrian that mayor
5. {Interviewer: "Fenty [Adrian Fenty was the DC mayor from whenever to whenever]."}
6. Fenty
7. That was his baby
8. And why would you have a trolley car when you have buses and a subway
9. you know
10. you see there at H Street is loaded with the tracks[56]
11. Trolley car [BARE NOUN] hadn't be– and they was [WAS LEVEL] trying to build that four or five years
12. They have the trolley– the tracks down there by the metro but um, by um Anacostia metro station
13. but the way the tro– the tracks are set up
14. It would be to carry people to um
15. Homeland Security
16. The back gate f– muf from off of that what's that
17. Four ninety-five
18. I don't know what it three-nine-f
19. that goes to Baltimore
20. So I don't know how that's going to work

Delores identifies several things that she finds problematic about the streetcar, and interestingly, money is not quite chief among them. As she goes further beyond her initial statement about the streetcar being a "money-wasting idea," she goes on to enumerate where the streetcar will travel. "They have the trolley– the tracks down there by the metro, but, um, by Anacostia metro station, but the way the tro– the tracks are set up, it would be to carry people to um Homeland Security."

She points out that the streetcar will begin at the Anacostia metro station. The metro station in Anacostia, a disembarkation point for the subway that runs under the Anacostia River and into the neighborhood, is actually quite a distance from the center of the neighborhood, which is most commonly understood to be the intersection of Martin Luther King Avenue and Good Hope Road. It takes a six-block walk, past abandoned buildings and Thurgood Marshall School, to get from the Anacostia metro station to the center of the neighborhood, so transit from the station is a good thing. However, then, she says *but* (line 13).

This *but* is a significant conjunction, as it sets up a contrast between where the tracks are and where they are headed. A route for any transportation line meant to serve the people of the neighborhood would therefore likely run along MLK toward Good Hope and have the added benefit of serving people who come by car or by foot across the Eleventh Street bridge, which ends at the MLK/Good Hope intersection.

Meanwhile, the move of the offices of the Department of Homeland Security (DHS) has been touted as an opportunity to bring some people into Southeast who do not otherwise live and work there, perhaps increasing homeownership in Anacostia and bringing people to patronize the businesses there. However, the streetcar is poised to bring people not from the metro station into the heart of the neighborhood, where they will be able to shop and take part in the community, but as a means to allowing the people who work at DHS to avoid interacting with people in the neighborhood. Because there are already bus lines that run the route from the metro station to the St. Elizabeth's campus, where DHS is to be headquartered, the streetcar is unabashedly redundant—its only possible use could be to allow a certain segment of the population to avoid having to ride the bus.

The streetcar, therefore, serves as a proxy for "improvement" to the neighborhood that ultimately does not serve the residents who live there. The streetcar does not run down MLK toward Good Hope, nor does it run up Morris Road toward the schools, the community center, and the Anacostia Community Museum. It is designed to take people from the metro station and whisk them as quickly as possible toward DHS, allowing the new employees who are meant to contribute to the community to instead avoid it entirely.

The people the streetcar will serve are not the residents of Anacostia, but the people who will come to work there—and who will be whisked from the subway, to their offices, and back to the subway, without having to interact with the community. To borrow a term from linguistic anthropology, for Delores the streetcar indexes, or comes to stand in for, this passing over of the community. It is not merely that it is a "money-wasting idea." It matters also for whom that money is being wasted—and it's not for the people of Anacostia.

When we look at this "why," it is easier to understand the "how" behind the forms that Delores uses. "They done had them trolley tracks laid down for five years; I haven't seen no trolley car run yet" carries two meanings. One is the surface meaning, that the streetcar project is a waste of money. But the second is that the streetcar represents something which is clearly "other": the people who will be in the neighborhood but who will use the streetcar to avoid becoming a part of it. And given the demographics of the rest of Washington compared to the demographics of Anacostia, the odds are that these others will be white. For Delores, enacting African American identity through her grammar when talking about the streetcar is a means of staking a claim against those who will eventually ride it—reinforcing the Blackness of her neighborhood as she discusses that which threatens it. Though Delores uses AAL grammatical features regularly in her speech, it is relatively rare to see several features clustered closely together. That she uses them here is reminiscent of Obama's "Nah, we straight": it's a sudden assemblage of grammar in one place for one purpose, which, if we look broadly, turns out to be the same as his.

Quantitative analysis shows us another layer of Black place-making through language. By diving into topic-based style-shifting, and understanding the attitudes buried within the things being talked about, we can come to understand why those topics cause these kinds of change. Repeatedly what we find are more and more versions of Delores's words—where the linguistic enactment of race serves to solidify the enactment of place. Anacostia, the language says, is a place where Blackness matters, and it is a place where Black language matters in talking about it.

## Notes

1. Alim and Smitherman, *Articulate while Black*, 14. Alim and Smitherman note a number of features of Black preacher rhetorical style employed by Obama in a variety of settings, including slower, more pointed cadence; repetition; reference to Bible verses in secular contexts; and circular narration style. Although this was not a particular point of analysis for this volume, this kind of Black rhetorical style is employed by several of the interview subjects, particularly Tana, whose repetitions were frequent as she emphasized various points in her sociolinguistic interview.

2. Many linguists have pointed out the importance of signifyin' in Black oral styles; the principal work is by Mitchell-Kernan, "Signifying and Marking." Signifyin' among adults has also been documented at length by Smitherman, *Talkin' That Talk*; among others by Alim, *You Know My Steez*; and among schoolchildren by Delfino, "Fighting Words?" and *Speaking of Race*. In signifyin' meaning is encoded principally with humorous, often insulting indirection, relying on the shared understanding between culturally Black speakers. Morgan ("African American Speech Community") in particular points out that signifyin' is highly dependent on social context and the existing power relations between speakers; in turn it also has the power to subvert them. In the case of Obama, Alim and Smitherman note that Obama engages in acts of signifyin' when he roasts other politicians such as Donald Trump (32) and in the further continuation of the Ben's Chili Bowl

encounter discussed here, when he goes on to ask for "real cheddar cheese, not that Velveeta stuff" (30). It is a principal way in which Obama exhibits his dexterity with the often extraordinarily subtle style shifts which allow him to become marked as a speaker who is distinctly representative of Black culture even as he moves through white spaces using standardized, white varieties of English.

3. Sabiyha Prince's anthropological study of gentrification in DC begins with the U Street corridor as a central motif. She explains how an encounter with a toy car being remotely controlled by a small white boy, who in years past would not have lived in the neighborhood, comes to symbolize the rapid change of the neighborhood as well as represent white indifference to Black presence there.

4. Scollon and Scollon, *Discourses in Place.*

5. Holliday, "Intonational Variation" and "Multiracial Identity"; Mitchell-Kernan, "Signifying and Marking"; Alim and Smitherman, *Articulate while Black*; DeBose, "African American Church Language."

6. Smitherman, "What Is Africa to Me?," 96.

7. Britt and Weldon, "African American English in the Middle Class"; Rahman, "Middle-Class African Americans"; Spears, "African-American Language Use"; and Taylor, "Response."

8. Baker-Bell, *Linguistic Justice,* 10.

9. Baker-Bell, 10. Baker-Bell also argues that the linguistic aspect of racism has been undertheorized in the scholarship belonging to critical race theory (CRT). See, e.g., Delgado and Stefancic, *Critical Race Theory.* I agree with this point and argue that it works both ways: CRT has been underutilized as an explanatory model in sociolinguistics, and the effects of language as a site of racial injustice have been undertheorized in CRT overall. See also Grieser, "Critical Race Theory."

10. Eckert and Rickford, *Style and Sociolinguistic Variation.*

11. This feature, known as *rhoticity,* is variable in a number of American English varieties, most notably the New York variety, which Labov, in *Social Stratification*, studied and which formed the bases for his attention-to-speech theory of style-shifting.

12. Labov, *Language in the Inner City* and *Social Stratification.*

13. Labov, *Language in the Inner City* and *Social Stratification*; Shuy, Wolfram, and Riley, *Field Techniques*; Fasold, *Tense Marking in Black English.*

14. Trudgill "Sex, Covert Prestige"; and Kiesling, "Men's Identities." See also Campbell-Kibler, "I'll Be the Judge" and "Accent, (ING)," for detailed

explorations of social perception of this variable; and Eckert, "Variation and the Indexical Field," for a discussion of this variable's indexicality.

15. Campbell-Kibler, "I'll Be the Judge" and "Accent, (ING)"; Eckert, "Variation and the Indexical Field."

16. *Ebonics* is a term which dates to 1973, from a conference of psychologists who were seeking a name for the variety of English spoken by African Americans. A combination of "ebony" and "phonics," the term was meant to invoke a positive association between the speech style and the group that used it. In 1996 the term was used by the Oakland (California) Unified School District in a resolution to recognize its heavily African American student population's native variety of speech and to seek funding to develop programs to help students bridge between Ebonics and the privileged white variety spoken by their teachers. For several reasons this resolution exploded in the news with a great deal of backlash, mostly representing misunderstandings of the variety and the resolution. Since then, professional linguists have often distanced from the term. Baugh, *Beyond Ebonics*; Rickford, *African American Vernacular*; and Rickford and Rickford, *Spoken Soul*, provide accessible explanations of the controversy, the backlash, and the naming issues that resulted.

17. That Lucy uses "marketplace" is actually quite interesting, given the idea of the linguistic marketplace, which was most prominently introduced by Sankoff and Laberge in "Linguistic Market." It refers to speakers who hold jobs where language use is central, such as teachers or receptionists, and who are expected to use more and more of the standardized (white) variety.

18. This kind of close following study is, however, very fruitful for the study of individual variation. For instance, see Podesva's work on intonation in "Phonation Type" and "Salience and the Social Meaning."

19. Many of the foundational studies in the field of sociolinguistics rest on the study of AAL. Labov's work in New York City, Wolfram's work in Detroit, and Wolfram's work with Ralph Fasold's work in Washington, DC, are all important early studies of AAL. Rickford documents the variety in great detail in *African American Vernacular English;* his general audience book with Russell Rickford, *Spoken Soul*, proves an accessible introduction to the variety and its social significance. Green's *African American English* is the foundational work on the syntactic phenomena of African American English and provides a formal syntactic analysis of the variety. Thomas's article "Phonological and Phonetic Characteristics of African American English" provides a detailed explanation of the variety's distinct phonology.

20. The work of many linguists who work in language and educational disparities make this point, including Charity Hudley and Mallinson, *Understanding English Language Variation* and *We Do Language*; Flores and Rosa, "Undoing Appropriateness"; and Paris, *Language across Difference*.

21. Craig and Washington, "Grade-Related Changes"; Van Hofwegen, "Apparent-Time Evolution"; Van Hofwegen and Wolfram, "Coming of Age" and "On the Utility of Composite Indices."

22. Kohn et al., *African American Language: Language.*

23. Bailey and Cukor-Avila, "Rural Texas."

24. Lisa Green has offered many of these very valid critiques in her books on African American English acquisition and in other works such as Seymour, Bland-Stewart, and Green, "Difference versus Deficit." A countervailing opinion is offered by Van Hofwegen and Wolfram in "On the Utility of Composite Indices." I agree in part with perspectives offered by each of these authors. My aim here is to point out what DDM does offer in terms of examining style-shifting across multiple speakers and I argue for its utility in this specific application only.

25. There are a few notable exceptions to this, such as the loss of /r/ in Northeast varieties or the merger of front lax vowels before nasals, called the PIN/PEN merger, in Southern English. Generally when phonology is overtly commented on, it is highly enregistered, that is, agreed on by people as indexing a particular group.

26. Wolfram, *Sociolinguistic Description*; Fasold, *Tense Marking in Black English*; Labov, *Language in the Inner City*; and Rickford and Mc-Nair-Knox, "Style Shift."

27. Weldon, "Middle Class African American Language" and *Middle Class African American English;* Spears, "African-American Language Use" and "African American Standard English"; and Rickford and Price, "Girlz II Women."

28. Craig and Washington, "Grade-Related Changes" and *Malik Goes to School*; and Renn and Terry, "Operationalizing Style." These authors show that similar results are obtained whether a "features per numbers of words" approach or a "features per intonation unit" approach is taken. For the interviews in the present book, the average words per intonation unit was used as the benchmark for the DDM.

29. Chafe, *Discourse, Consciousness, and Time.*

30. This is the same coding procedure I used in my work on topic-based shifting in the Corpus of Regional African American Language, where I

found very similar findings. See Grieser, "Investigating Topic-Based Style Shifting."

31. Rickford et al., "Rappin on the Copula Coffin."

32. See explanations in Labov, "Contraction, Deletion"; Wolfram, "Relationship"; Green, *African American English*; Rickford et al., "Rappin on the Copula Coffin."

33. Spears, "African American Standard English."

34. Hoover, "Community Attitudes."

35. Question from the DCA subcorpus of the Corpus of Regional African American English. See also Fasold, *Tense Marking in Black English.*

36. Labov explains these motivations further in his 1984 work on sociolinguistic fieldwork, and his 2012 revisiting of the use of topic in making coding decisions about formal and informal language is instructive. Baugh's response paper in the same volume raises questions about the enterprise of sociolinguistic interviewing more broadly and the role topic plays, especially for already marginalized speakers who are often the subject of linguistic study.

37. Becker, "Sociolinguistic Interview." Becker argues that in the absence of this topic/module format, we are doing something other than sociolinguistic interviewing. I refer to this topic/question-based form as the "classic sociolinguistic interview."

38. Bell, "Language Style as Audience Design" and "Back in Style."

39. Rickford and McNair-Knox, in their study of Foxy Boston, an African American teenager in Palo Alto, California, argue that her speech showed significant differences in rates of usage of morphosyntactic markers of African American Language based on whether she was talking to an unfamiliar, older, white interviewer or talking to an African American interviewer with whom she was familiar (McNair-Knox), or talking to that interviewer's daughter, who was one of Foxy's friends. However, they also showed a significant intersection between interviewer and topic. Macaulay, in "Question of Genre," points out that if one uses topic to identify equivalent parts of white interviewer and Black interviewer interviews in the Foxy Boston data, then "there is no style shifting and no audience effect" (82).

40. Grieser, "Locating Style," "Investigating Topic-Based Style Shifting," and "Two Sides."

41. Kendall and Farrington, "Corpus of Regional African American Language." See also Grieser, "Investigating Topic-Based Style Shifting."

42. My favorite such interview is that of Amy, a woman in her eighties, with whom I sat down in her kitchen to do a half-hour interview. I left her

home five hours later, after recording two hours with her alone and two hours with her daughter, Vee (and having been served tuna casserole for dinner).

43. Labov, "Anatomy of Style-Shifting." Labov suggests that this actually constitutes two separate topics with respect to linguistic analysis—that the first intonation unit, in which the speaker is replying to the interviewer's question directly, should be considered differently than any further discussion that follows.

44. Strauss and Corbin, *Grounded Theory.*

45. Labov, "Anatomy of Style-Shifting," 91–92.

46. Several linguists have questioned the efficacy of the attention-to-speech model as a predictor of variation. For example: Wolfson, "Speech Events"; and Baugh, "Dissection," his response to Labov's decision tree.

47. This is the same method I used in work with older data available on the Corpus of Regional African American Language (CORAAL), where I found a similar pattern of style-shifting based on the social indexes of the topic being discussed. See Grieser, "Investigating Topic-Based Style Shifting."

48. A chi-square test for topic is significant ($X^2(12, N = 18863) = 58.557$, $p< .001$), and a multivariate regression shows that topic is a significant predictor of a change in rate ($F (13, 18662) = 4.344, p < .01$, $R^2 = .002$).

49. Anderson, "Justifying Race Talk."

50. For example, one might look to work on the roles that AAL styles play in African American Women's Language; see Lanehart, *African American Women's Language*; Morgan, "African American Speech Community" and "African American Women's Language"; and Mitchell-Kernan, "Signifying and Marking" and "Signifying, Loud-Talking and Marking"; in men's language (Kirkland, "Black Masculine Language"); in Black-identified biracial identities (Holliday, "Intonational Variation" and "Multiracial Identity"); or in multiracial settings (Rosa, *Looking like a Language*; and Paris, *Language across Difference*). Especially instructive is the body of work on middle-class African American English, which breaks the long-standing myth that AAL is primarily a language style of the working class and which instead reveals its use to signal racial identity in contrast to standardized English varieties which are usually associated with higher socioeconomic status. See, for example, Weldon, *Middle Class African American English*, and most work by Arthur Spears.

51. Grieser, "Investigating Topic-Based Style Shifting."

52. Gumperz, *Discourse Strategies.*

53. Alim, Rickford, and Ball, "Introduction," in *Raciolinguistics.*

54. District of Columbia, *Transit Alternatives Analysis.*

55. The Washington Metropolitan Area Transit Authority uses a network of fifty-eight drainage pumping systems throughout the system, which together remove 3 million gallons a day.

56. The H Street NE streetcar finally opened in 2016, five years behind schedule. At the time of this writing it has been plagued with delays and accidents and is still considered an overspend.

# Chapter 4

# "Greater than Any Gift"

## Race, Geography, and Agency East of the River

In the spring of 2016 a small bus crossed the newly renovated Eleventh Street bridge into the heart of Anacostia at Martin Luther King Boulevard and Good Hope Road. Aboard it were a dozen businesspeople expecting to take a tour of areas ripe for potential future development. Billed as a "Space Finding Tour," the trip, sponsored by *Washington Business Journal* and the Washington, DC, Economic Partnership, aimed to show to investors sites for potential development along the Anacostia River, including the riverfront near the Washington Nationals Stadium, Sheridan Station, and MLK Avenue.[1]

As the bus made its way down Martin Luther King Avenue, approximately a dozen protestors met it, holding signs reading "Stop This Gentrification Bus" and "Stop Displacement . . . Don't Move," and "#OccupyBarryFarms." The protestors successfully delayed the bus for nearly half an hour before the police were summoned. The officers asked the bus to reverse course, but not before arresting one protestor.

The residents of Anacostia have a name for this kind of tour: the "Hood Safari." A representative of Empower DC, a membership-based community organization, objected both to the tour and its use of the word *space*: "[Our] members perceive WDEP's 'Space Finding Tour' as a kind of Gentrification Safari. The name alone points to a profound insensitivity to the predominately low-income black residents who call these neighborhoods home. This is not space. This is a community. The city and developers believe the community could be 'better' with more development, restaurants, higher-income people. It is our job to ask: Better for who?"[2]

Central to the exploration principle of this book is the process by which space is claimed. I argue that in the face of encroaching gentrification, the linguistic means of staking space claims, which I have named the "linguistic practices of place," are both a crucial part of the process of making a space belong to the residents of a neighborhood and means of counteracting the legitimacy of gentrification. Yet across the United States, the history of discriminatory housing practices such as redlining proves that space continues to bear witness to centuries of overt and covert racism. This is especially true in Washington, DC, where a history of radical Black success is built on top of a landscape that still bears the marks of the slave trade and historic racial struggle.

I collected data for this project at a time of major demographic change in Washington, the moment when, for the first time since 1970, DC's African American majority had tipped to a plurality, with residents claiming a non-Black identity together making up over fifty percent of the population.[3] Due to this shift, the meaning of DC as a Black space is changing, and this comes through in how Anacostians talk about the ways their neighborhood is racialized and re-racialized. The changes to the racial demographics of Washington mean that the reputation of Anacostia as Black space is also changing, with profound implications for the ways that African Americans continue to live in the nation's capital at the outset of the twenty-first century.

While Chocolate Cities provide a means for Black belonging, white control over space continues to be the predominant way that Americans of all races experience the physical landscape. It is mostly white developers who board a small bus to come into the neighborhood center, and mostly white dollars which often determine the ways neighborhoods like Anacostia are permitted to change. Yet one finds that such control is both covertly and overtly rejected. Here, again, the linguistic practices of place serve to make real a racial geography which names DC as Black space, and within DC specifically, Anacostia; the invocation of Black middle-class success in turn maps Black success onto Black space. When Black success is mapped onto the space, it changes the demands residents can make about their neighborhood—claiming agency and insisting on a partnership that develops a neighborhood for them. These mappings serve as a means of metaphorically blocking the gentrification bus and changing what developers see as mere "space" into Black community.

## East of the River, West of the Park: Naming and Racializing Space

In chapter 1, I showed how first-person deixis serves to unify Washington's Black community and, in turn, mark the entirety of Washington, DC, as space for that Black community. However, even at its peak number of Black population, the city was just under 30 percent people of other races (mostly white), and that number has been rapidly changing. While DC may be claimed as Black space, within it has always also contained white space against which Black space is contrasted.

Returning to the concept of fractal recursivity is useful here:[4] distinctions made at one scale are recursively overlaid onto larger scales and smaller scales. In the case of the racialization of the city, DC is marked as Black space in contrast to the rest of the United States and other cities; then within DC, the Southeast Quadrant is recursively marked as Black space within the city; then Anacostia, and particular parts of Anacostia, are marked as Black spaces within Southeast. These recursive contrasts allow residents to make ever more fine-grained distinctions, which in turn lay claim to particular spaces as belonging to them.

"If you look at the city in thirds," Thomas says, "this is one-third of it. But there's another third of it, which is the middle part, then there's a another third. Um, and these are rough numbers by the way. But the other third is the part that's, you know, west of the park, for example. They– that term is often used."

Thomas, a communications professional in his forties, is heavily involved in a variety of projects in Anacostia. When he explained the geography of the city, he placed names on sections that I had not yet heard. While "East of the River" is a commonly applied moniker for the neighborhood of Anacostia and its nearby surrounds, "West of the Park" is quite a bit less commonly used. The park in this instance is Rock Creek Park, the large greenspace controlled by the National Park Service that cuts through the middle of Washington's Northwest Quadrant and winds north from the Potomac River into Maryland. It cuts behind the exclusive neighborhood of Kalorama, where the Obama family moved when they left the White House, and separates many other affluent neighborhoods in Northwest from less affluent but recently gentrifying neighborhoods like Columbia Heights. These neighborhoods were among the scant handful to retain a white majority during the heyday of DC's Black population in the 1970s, and DC's white residents commonly use "west of the park" to delineate the parts of the Northwest Quadrant that are seen as more ethnically and socioeconomically diverse from areas typically viewed as the bedrock of white exclusionary tactics.[5] Wards 3 and 4, both west of Rock Creek, have some of the fewest units of affordable housing in the District, with new affordable construction almost nonexistent.[6]

DC residents also often use "west of the park" to talk about investments in the city and the policies that certain areas permit. Thomas talked about the area in terms of the kinds of policies in which the city was willing to invest:

> I think what happens is when when people are thinking about policy when they're thinking about, um, you know, them versus those. They begin to geographically differentiate between the

s– they pull out that geography to talk about differences. I think perceived mostly, but in some cases real, uh, differences in how the city is . . . How the residents are treated, how the city responds to these different parts of town. So that, I mean, that is my under-standing of how it's ["west of the park"] used.

Giving a space a name is one way to make clear the rela-tionships between that space and other spaces, as suggested in chapter 1 regarding the renaming of the neighborhood surround-ing Gallaudet University as "NoMa" (NOrth of MAssachusetts Av-enue). Names, as Thomas points out, differentiate spaces, making visible their differences.

In the same way that East of the River has nearly always had a strong African American majority—even when the city was at its peak African American population, the areas west of the park were far beyond majority white, with the reported "negro" popu-lation in the low single digit percentages—naming this area "west of the park" allows residents to call attention to the racial divide in the city without doing so explicitly, in much the same way that "east of the river" can be used to call attention to what others in the city might consider problems. Thomas goes on to point out that he hears "east of the river" used "when you were thinking about the fact that this side of town has so many more challenges than the other sides of town, or how, uh, development has eluded you know, this side of the river, so to speak, in favor of everything that's in the center and western part of town. So it's always to me in a policy connotation or something that invokes the stark differences between this side of town and another side of town."

These "stark differences," of course, center not only on ameni-ties available to residents and the investments the city makes in their areas, but also on the differences in the races of those who inhabit them. DC becomes understood in terms of the ways it is chopped up—into east and west, into white and Black.

East of the River, therefore, and particularly Anacostia itself is usually understood as Black space, with older Anacostians like Gus being quick to point out that Anacostia is "home to the largest population of Blacks in the city over here, right over here. And people say well, 'You know there's some that live up in Northwest,' yeah okay, that's good. But they far and few between. I'm talking about large influx, you know, generations."

Another place where Blackness is specifically projected onto the space of Anacostia is in the outreach of the Anacostia Community Museum. Until the opening of the National African American History Museum on the Washington Mall in September 2016, the mission of the ACM was distinctively racial in nature, as Porter, the museum employee introduced earlier, points out:

> When we first started out . . . we were down on Martin Luther King Junior Avenue. Heavily foot, trafficked area. And at that time, of course, our mission was to serve the, uh, African American community. We were for all intents and purposes the Smithsonian's outreach vehicle to the Black community. Because up until that time, there was not one. So we were it. And that was our original mission: explore issues, uh, related to African American art history and culture.

The original location of the museum, on the main thoroughfare of the neighborhood, made it a prime location for outreach to the DC African American community, and until very recently it served as the de facto African American history museum, with its mission focused on the Washington African American community.[7]

That the location of the museum makes it the "outreach vehicle" to the African American community underscores the ways in which the Anacostia community is synonymous with the African American community: the physical space of Anacostia, by the time the museum opened its doors in 1967, was indistinguishable from African American identity. This has remained relatively unchanged, at least in Porter's view: "Because of our location we can't forsake the African-American community. So we wanna make sure that we also provide some programming that is going to be of interest to them—to our local constituency."

Statements like these project African Americanness onto the physical space of Anacostia specifically, and the neighborhoods east of the river more generally. Yet there is a none-too-small irony in the fact that the Anacostia neighborhood's name has come to stand for all of Southeast and all of Washington, DC. This is because, moving down a level in distinctions, "Anacostia" used to be the white area of what Washingtonians now refer to as being "Anacostia."

When older residents discuss the ways that the neighborhood is integrated, they are rejecting the positioning that the neighborhood is undesirable because it is all African American and that the residents are unwelcoming to white Washingtonians. This description, however, mostly applied to their discussions about white residents who were moving in during the 2010s and not to discussions of the ways that Anacostia has historically been segregated. For instance, when Delores talks about the history of Anacostia, she points out the historical boundaries on the space:

> You know how you make the turn to come up Hill Street? The street before you get there. Treetop Street? That big stree– hill. That was the line. White people were on that street, and we were on this street. And that we were– it was Black from here to Portland Street, and from Portland Street to the District line was white. So literally white people came through the Black neighborhood to go home. Black people came through the white neighborhood to go home. I mean that's the way it was. Crossing each other's neighborhoods to go home, but not living– not living integ– together.

Gus takes this even further. In a portion of his interview in which he explains what the neighborhood was like when he was a child, he says,

> I remember the golf course down there [by the river]. [It] took up, uh, two sides of the park. The front nine and the back nine on the other side of the bridge. You had to walk up underneath there and go on the other side. And that was predominantly white. You know, the Anacostia swimming pool was predominantly white. The only place we could go was up at Francis.[8] That's up in Georgetown. That that that that was before the the great Integration.

Later in the interview he has even more to offer about who lived in Anacostia when he was growing up. As he describes having to sit in the back of the movie theater on MLK Avenue, he offers,

> Anacostia was all white. You know I remember when it wasn't nothing but a lot of woods out here. You know, people didn't have places to go. This used to be– all Anacostia per se was all– all-white community. It was all white. And you– you know you couldn't walk around. You know you had Barry Farms, you had, uh, you know you had other places, uh, I– can't remember. Stewart Road and all that. But this– Anacostia was all white.

In pointing out Black spaces such as Barry Farm, even as he is asserting Anacostia's whiteness Gus is also asserting that it was racially mixed, albeit extremely segregated.[9] This distinction between the white and Black areas of Southeast Washington is yet another example of the ways in which discourses about the neighborhood are fractally recursive: the same racial binary that divides space in Washington, DC, is projected onto the smaller domain of Anacostia itself.

For interviewees of all ages, the idea that the geography of Washington generally, and of Anacostia specifically, is a racialized geography is a constant refrain. The process of dividing space into white space and Black space, then ascribing names to those spaces, as Robert does in talking about west of the park and east of the river, is a means of emphasizing the racialization of the physical experience of Washington, DC. It also serves a second purpose, however. When the city and the neighborhoods within it are racially marked, it opens the door for certain physical spaces to be understood firmly as African American space. This has significant ramifications for understandings of ownership and agency, which I turn to next.

### "I Saw My People Everywhere": Black Space, Black Success

Long before Parliament-Funkadelic put the label of Chocolate City on the District, the area was already known as a place of great opportunity for African Americans. This reputation drove the influx of people like Mr. Moore, who came to the city looking for opportunities unavailable in the civil rights–era South:

> I came with the attitude saying that if you cannot make it in Washington as an African American male, as an African American person, as an African American individual, you can't make it anywhere in the world as a– as a black person. Why? Because you had everything to your– at your disposal. All the educational institutions. All the free information from what do you call it– the libraries. And you had all– even if you didn't know, um, how to go out and purchase a house, you had access to the knowledge to do it. See that was the thing. Washington gave Black people access to whatever. And that to me as was greater than any gift that anybody could give.

The drawing of distinctions between white and Black areas happens on a small scale, when residents talk about Uniontown and Hillsdale within Anacostia, on a larger scale when Black residents mark all of Southeast Washington as a place for African Americans, and on an even larger scale still when they mark DC as a whole and as a Chocolate City, in contrast to the white United States. These delineations of Black spaces within white spaces, whether at the whole-country level or on the single-city-block level, don't simply identify Black spaces, however. They identify spaces that make Black success possible.

"[In my hometown, when I went out] and went anywhere I would see all these white people," says Amelia, a resident in her fifties who has lived in DC since early adulthood. "But in DC when I went downtown, I saw when I left home, it was Black. When I got downtown, it was Black. When I went uptown, it was Black. You know, so I saw my people everywhere. Everywhere! Working positions and jobs that, um that just didn't happen in [the city I came from]. It just wasn't like that." Like Mr. Moore, Amelia frames Washington as a place of opportunity, where African Americans now hold jobs that African Americans could not have held in the city she grew up in. What is most powerful here, however, is the repetitive syntax she uses to emphasize the ways that African Americans were all over the city. Her repetition of the structure "When I [left home/got downtown/went uptown], it was Black" serves to highlight the ubiquity of the Black presence in the space. Her repetition of the structure serves to focus on the three locations—home, downtown, and uptown—and emphasizes that wherever she went, she saw "her people."

The use of personal deixis that unites DC's African American community works similarly in Amelia's quote: in referring to "my people," she refers to the entire DC Black community. This works with her use of the repetitive structure to emphasize all the places where she sees this community, reinforcing the idea of DC as a space of Black welcome.

Through these connections, Black Washingtonians mark DC as Black space. Lucy, the schoolteacher introduced in chapter 1, similarly focuses on the ways that the opportunities afforded DC's African American population changed the socioeconomic makeup of that population:

> One thing about DC—and I didn't realize it until I started living other places—is that not only do we have a large number of African Americans in one city, but just kind of like the, um, I guess the economic make up of that amount of African Americans in one place where you do have um . . . abject poverty but you have like a lot of affluent African Americans. And when I've lived in other places usually the African American communities were the poorest in those communities and that's it. You didn't really see too many you know African Americans who were affluent or you know involved in, um, politics.

Like Amelia, Lucy compares Washington with other locales where she has lived (in Lucy's case, after she'd grown up in Washington) and focuses on the ways that Washington is different because of the varied socioeconomic status of the African American community. Black Washingtonians are not merely the "poorest in those communities" but instead, can be affluent. Sally, a generation older than Lucy, explains why that is, when she points out that she's part of "the first generation of black people to go to college en masse, and to have those government jobs, nonfactory jobs en masse." The marking of DC as Black space, therefore, serves an important purpose. It sets DC apart from other locations where Washingtonians experienced segregation, discrimination, and lack of opportunity, and instead, marks it as a place where Black Americans can thrive.

When Black residents talk about Washington, they refer to it as being space which is first and foremost for Black people. At the same time, Southeast emerges as a space especially set apart for Black Washingtonians. As Washington begins to change, the preservation of this Black space is paramount, as Justin, Lucy's colleague at the elementary school, makes clear: "Culturally, it seems like Ward 8, or Southeast, Anacostia is like the last, uh, bastion of of the African American community in the city. Or at least in many ways, it appears that way."

Marking Southeast DC as Black space has ramifications for how residents stake their claims on it. Residents like Lucy, Amelia, and Mr. Moore challenge the links made by many white Americans between African Americans and social class: in a Black space like Washington, they argue, African Americans experience success and socioeconomic mobility. Like the racial divisions seen in the geography, the link between the ideas of Black space and Black success in Washington writ large is fractally recursive: if Washington is a large Black space where African Americans experience success, then this effect is only intensified in Southeast. This, in turn, has important ramifications for the ways residents are able to claim agency in the neighborhood: if Blackness is success, then the neighborhood must be seen not as a place to be rehabilitated but instead as a place where already successful residents rightfully insist on exerting agency over the ways their neighborhood is changing.

## Doing Black Development

On a weekday afternoon I sit in a private study room at the Anacostia Neighborhood Branch Library located on Good Hope Road. Renovated by the city in 2010 as part of a campaign to bring the city's libraries to twenty-first-century standards, the Anacostia Library, like other branch libraries around the city, is a hub of city services wrapped in a designer facade.[10] The wide windows allow sunlight to stream into the room and across the library floor and a glass wall opens the view to the mature trees of Good Hope Road and onto streets lined with many of DC's iconic rowhouses.

The library is full of people even in the middle of the day. At the time I began collecting data there were few spaces in the neighborhood available to work with a laptop and wifi—the lone coffee shop was located inside of a grocery store, and the Anacostia Arts Center, with its wide open workspaces and brunch and coffee shop, would not open until two years into my research in 2013. As a result, I spent many hours in the library.

Anacostians fill the seats at tables with computers, browsing the *Washington Post,* using job sites, or surfing social media. Throughout the day the loudspeaker occasionally erupts with an announcement—the DC Public Schools summer lunch program will begin downstairs in half an hour, volunteers will be meeting people in the main conference room to provide tax filing assistance starting at 1:00 p.m., and so on. The library, like most DC libraries, seems to sit on the precipice of local change; on the one hand, serving a community whose members need assistance with finding food, and on the other, being a technologically advanced architectural marvel in the middle of the neighborhood.

The library represents a neighborhood space that works. City investments into the neighborhood like the library are clearly directed at the neighborhood's existing residents, as the variety of social services incorporated into the library's various spaces indicate. When the city began its investment into the Anacostia Branch Library, the library was operating out of a double-wide trailer. Building a new facility demonstrated a commitment from the city to its goals of increasing reading literacy and digital literacy among the DC population. The library has become Anacostian space; it is filled with residents during the day and early afternoon. It serves people of all social classes: people who live in the neighborhood's family shelter are equally as welcome as those who live in the expensive new gated-community rowhouses up the street.

It is here where I borrowed a room to interview Robert about his involvement in various aspects of the neighborhood, including his work with the new Eleventh Street Bridge Park project that I will discuss more fully in the next section. The park will provide a fresh outdoor space for neighborhood gatherings and serve as a pedestrian-accessible connector between Anacostia and Capitol Hill on the other side of the river. Yet many Anacostians, both those involved in making the project happen and those watching from the sidelines, worry that such an amenity will make living near the park more attractive, thus driving up housing costs and making the community by the river unaffordable for the people who already live there.

None of my interviewees disagree that improvements to their neighborhood continue to be necessary. But the kind of improvements matters to them. Bridge Park and the library represent two different kinds of development within Anacostia. Both are examples of massive investments from the city and both are largely community-driven. Yet at the same time, the library unabashedly serves the neighborhood as it is: serving food when the schools are closed, offering tax-filing assistance. Meanwhile, Bridge Park project seems poised to potentially change the nature of the neighborhood by creating new spaces. In other words, only one of the two seems likely to drive gentrification.

DC's racialized wealth gap is evident even when my interviewees talk about seeing DC as a place of great Black opportunity and frame and reframe Anacostia as a place where the Black middle class has always been present. They talk about the socioeconomic strength of the neighborhood much like they do about encroaching white people—that is, despite demographics that say otherwise. The DC Economic Strategy Plan, which Mayor Muriel Bowser developed, shows that despite the large number of Black-identifying DC residents, the mean and median salaries of Black residents is only a fraction of its white residents.[11] In 2014 the median income for a Black DC household was $40,000, compared to a median of $131,000 for a white household, rising to $44,000 and $156,000, respectively, by 2016. These numbers in turn reflect the disparity between the median salaries in the various wards: from 2005 to 2009, Ward 3, a West of the Park area with the highest white population in the District, had a median household income of $97,690 and a mean household income of $109,909; whereas East of the River, Ward 7's median income was $34,965 and its mean was $39,828, and Ward 8 had a median of $31,188 and a mean of $31,643.

At the same time, Wards 7 and 8 are directly adjacent to Prince George's County with its unparalleled concentration of African American wealth. When middle-class Black residents fled these wards during the early 1970s, they could more easily move over the line into Maryland because of Suitland Parkway. Built at the end of World War II to connect Camp Springs in Maryland with Bolling Air Force Base (now Joint Base Andrews and Joint Base Anacostia-Bolling, respectively) and expedite the transfer of troops and equipment between the two bases, the parkway quickly became a commuter hub in the 1960s and 1970s. Former residents of the District could move quickly between new homes in Maryland and their well-paying government jobs. Because of the racial makeup of the Southeast Quadrant, many of the people who utilized the Suitland Parkway to move outside the District were African American.

The 2010 census data gives the population of PG County as 64 percent Black or African American alone, compared to 26 percent white alone, and 18 percent Hispanic (all other races were represented at 1 percent or less). The median household income in PG County for the 2012–2016 period was nearly $75,925. In the wake of the 2008 financial crash there has been a marked racial difference in the rebound of housing wealth in PG County, with African Americans experiencing very little recovery compared to their white neighbors.[12]

Because of PG County's close proximity to Washington, some of the first people to relocate into Anacostia were Black middle-class residents from PG County, making the question of what entailed gentrification—as opposed to what entailed change and investment—muddier than it might have been otherwise. For instance, one former city council candidate, Charles Wilson, when interviewed for the *Washington Post*, said, "I used to think it [gentrification] was about race—when white people moved into a black neighborhood. Then, I looked up the word. It's when a middle-class person moves into a poor neighborhood. And I realized: I am a gentrifier. I couldn't believe it. I don't like that word. It makes so many people uncomfortable."[13] In chapter 1 I discussed how the erasure of Black gentrification and the connection of white identity with gentrification means that people like Wilson fail to see themselves as being part of the reason the neighborhood is changing. But it more problematically erases the agentive creation of Black space, making the change processes happening in the neighborhood more about racial shift than about deepening the ways in which Black Anacostians can be part of their neighborhood.

When residents talk about the ways that their neighborhood is changing, it is often with reference to this kind of outsider change. A major concern, which I have highlighted in previous chapters, is displacement. This was particularly acute during the time of this research, as the recently funded Barry Farm project was displacing the residents of the existing affordable units, some of whom, their neighbors worried, would not move back, as was common in other parts of the city. For example, Kiesha points out that:

> The people of other ethnic groups coming to the, the what we consider the projects, the hood and tell people, "Oh we wanna fix up your neighborhood or whatever, we gonna, um, renovate so we need you to move out temporarily so we can fix up," and those people not thinking that "Okay we're gonna move out temporarily," but when they finish renovating, the people can't afford it, what they just fixed up and those people are moving to Prince George's county.

It is worth noting that Kiesha talks about this displacement as being the handiwork of "people of other ethnic groups" who come in, paralleling the general pattern of racializing the process of gentrification. It is further interesting that in her use of constructed dialogue, Kiesha is able to give voice to both sides of the issue by having both the developers she voices and the residents talk about it as "move[ing] out temporarily." Then she sets up the bait and switch: when the renovations are finished, "the people can't afford it, what they just fixed up."

In chapter 3 Delores's comments about the streetcar and its being to "carry people up to Homeland Security" are centrally about development, that the streetcar is not meant for the people of Anacostia. I explored how the deployment of AAL morphosyntax plays a crucial role in the subtle negotiation of rejecting this kind of development.[14] Others of her neighbors, however, are much less subtle with their rejection. Consider Amelia:

> We think we doing something so especially over here in Southeast, oh my god they have these these nonprofiteers. That's what they– I wanna say nonprofit but it's the nonprofit-E-E-R-S that'll come up with this great thing for– "This is what we're doing, This is for the young people blah blah in the summertime or the winter." They'll have this one affair, and after this one affair, they get their money. They got it's one affair. You don't hear from them no more until the next year it's never ongoing.

Here Amelia is directly criticizing not just infrastructure development but also program development and the ways in which money is invested into the community for one-time gains on the part of the organizations. She uses the coinage *nonprofiteers* to describe these people, and to make sure that I understand the blend, spells it out: nonprofit-E-E-R-S. In blending *nonprofit* and *profiteer* she is able to point out the direction of the benefit: while there might be a slight benefit to the community in terms of a summer program, in the end the gain is for the companies and not for the community.

This isn't to say that all development is automatically criticized. Development for the community is the goal, and when it does happen, residents notice and, especially if they are middle-class residents, praise it. For instance, Tracey, the ANC member, frames the changes happening in Anacostia with respect to her ability to find amenities:

> There are places to sit down and eat. One of the biggest– the good changes– I think, changes I've seen in the city, uh, is the development. It's alarming. When I moved here as a teacher the only place to sit down and eat in Anacostia or anywhere near Anacostia outside of carry-out, which I don't really think those are places that we would sit down and eat but, um, comfortably, was Subway. There's a Subway and then our other option was going to M Street in Navy Yard. And there was a Sizzling Express– Sizzler Express. But we only had forty-five minutes for lunch. So we literally [had] to go in and pick something up, and run back and scarf it down in ten minutes before we started teaching again. There are so many more places you can sit down and eat now um in Anacostia

Oliver, another teacher, echoes this same experience and also reflects:

> Now you getting sit-down restaurants off Cappers, so, you know Cappers was huge housing project you know right where the military, or the marine barracks is now and what, it took them two years to knock that whole thing down and now you look over there and it's you know one of those situations housing that the people that lived there before can't afford and you know the restaurants that they're bringing into those areas. It's– normally you have a McDonald's or KFC or you know all fast food now you getting sit down restaurants and you know places that you know [*laughter*] uh, sushi.

Tracey and Oliver demonstrate two different ways of framing the creation of new sit-down restaurants in the neighborhood. For Tracey the new restaurants represent places for Anacostians to be proud of: she later goes on to talk about how she has a place she can invite her friends to engage in the quintessential DC activity of Sunday brunch. Tracey contrasts the present situation of restaurants in Anacostia with the inconvenience she and her fellow teachers faced by not having these sorts of amenities: they had to "pick something up and scarf it down" because there was no place to buy food except across the river. By foregrounding the difficulty that she and her fellow teachers faced in finding food during their lunch break, Tracey frames the creation of new restaurants in Anacostia as a positive development that would have benefited her former teacher self.[15]

For Oliver, by contrast, new restaurants represent something quite different, though it should be noted that the developments Oliver is talking about are still across the Anacostia River, an area referred to by developers and city planners as "Near Southeast" or "Navy Yard." He makes specific mention of the redevelopment of "Cappers," which refers to the Arthur Capper public housing project in Southeast DC.[16] In the early 2000s the existing housing at the site was torn down and replaced with mixed-use development, which preserved the seven hundred low-income reserved units but also added upscale condominiums and new restaurants. But, Oliver notes, these aren't the usual restaurants that were previously in this area: not fast food places but sit-down places, and—as he laughs—sushi bars.

For Oliver the restaurants are not framed in terms of a previous difficulty but instead are presented *as* the difficulty—part of the unaffordability of the existing location. New restaurants are one way that the people who live in income-controlled housing are priced out of the area—even if they are able to afford their homes, thanks to the city, they are unable to afford to eat out. In addition, the housing itself no longer serves the community—it is "housing that the people that lived there before can't afford." That Oliver laughs and hedges with "you know" before saying "uh, sushi," marks his affective stance toward the new restaurants: he signals to the interviewer (and Lucy, his co-interviewee) that he thinks these restaurants are silly, which underscores his point about them being part of the new unaffordability of the neighborhood.

There is an inherent push-pull in the ways the residents of Anacostia talk about development. On the one hand things like new sit-down restaurants serve the neighborhood by providing places for residents to congregate and get different kinds of food quickly. Renovations of public spaces like the library provide places for services aimed at the residents of the neighborhood, bringing city services into the neighborhood and providing a place for Anacostians to congregate. But other places, like the new streetcar or the renovation of Barry Farm, are framed as being part of the decrease in affordability and as providing services that do not serve the neighborhood.

To determine what kinds of change actually *do* serve the neighborhood, it is necessary to look more carefully at the ways in which investments serve the community itself and the Black community more broadly.

**Flows East of the River**

At the root of the discussion about the ways that the neighborhood is changing are all the things that interviewees have talked about throughout this study: the long existence of the Black middle class in Anacostia, the safety of Black space in Anacostia, and the unparalleled opportunities provided to Black people in Washington, DC, generally and Anacostia specifically. Development, then, is couched in terms of what it gives to the existing Black community. Spaces like the library, which are unapologetically for the community, become spaces where development is welcome. But other spaces, like sushi restaurants and the unaffordable condominiums to which Lucy refers, become spaces that are racialized as white, regardless of the ability or inability of wealthier Black residents to afford them.

While residents invoke the existence of the Black middle class in Anacostia, they also say few people have disposable income—or they say people have disposable income but lack places to spend it east of the river. This is one of the problems Grey identifies when he talks about the ways that he feels the neighborhood is stalled:

> You ain't gonna make no money until you have some private industries coming in and trying to make some money. Then other private industries are coming. That's when, you know, you will grow a little bit. But as long as you just having this, you bring in government people now, and . . . you know they just work in, you know. They're not spend– you ain't gonna be able to spend money here where you make it, so. You can make it all day here, but you won't be able to spend it. And you have to go up. Go Northeast, Northwest somewhere else to en– you can't spend your money in Southeast. There's nowhere to spend your money in Southeast. So it would never grow. If you can't spend your money where you– where you live at.

One of the central changes anticipated during the time frame that I conducted the interviews for this book was the redevelopment of the former St. Elizabeth's Hospital site for the Department of Homeland Security (DHS) headquarters. St. Elizabeth's is a Southeast DC landmark, having opened in 1855 as one of the first psychiatric hospitals in Washington and one of the only to admit African Americans. It sits atop the hill just outside the boundary of Historic Anacostia and has sat empty, except for one wing, since 2010.

The development of St. Elizabeth's brings money into Southeast, in the form of the government contracts to refurbish the buildings, build roads to reach them, and even, as Delores points out, to build the streetcar to take people from the subway station to it. It will also bring over a number of new workers into Southeast, with the potential that some will buy homes there, though it is likely that many will commute and take advantage of new facilities like the streetcar to help them get to their offices.

The influx of government money can only go so far, however, as Grey points out. Government employees can come into the neighborhood, but "they just work" in the neighborhood. Without much private industry in the form of restaurants and shops, there are few places in Southeast for that money to go. Grey points out that the new workers "can make [money] all day here, but [they] won't be able to spend it." And without that expenditure, the neighborhood is unable to grow.

Grey's observation is interesting in part because he is part of the working class in Anacostia in his role as a school aide. Typically the expectation might be that those with different access to disposable income would feel differently about the need or ability to spend that income. However, that Anacostians desire a place to spend their money on their side of the river is a theme that is not at all sensitive to the socioeconomic status of the person being interviewed. Eli, for instance, the director of a major nonprofit that operates in Wards 7 and 8, echoes Grey's concerns:

> One of the reasons I feel like we haven't seen as much progress as we have is because we– we still don't have in mass numbers a lot of, um, good-paying jobs. I mean you have people who live east of the river who have good-paying jobs, but then they spend that disposable income close to where they work not you know back you know on this side and I think until we have that in mass numbers we're not going to see the same, um, speed of gentrification as you've seen in other parts of um, you know the city.

The idea that East of the River is a place where Black people need to be able to spend money is not a socioeconomic status–

related subject among the people who talk about it. Both professional and working-class interviewees talk about the need for this kind of investment. More tellingly, they discuss this investment explicitly in terms of the two sides of the river: that the issue is that people who live east of the river still have to spend their money west of it.

Residents talk about economic investment as being separated between east and west of the river. West of the river becomes the place where money flows and, despite the existence of and growing presence of African American wealth east of the river, in their telling there are no places to invest back into the community. It is only within this frame, when they consider that gentrification may provide investment opportunities for their own community in their own community, that residents talk about gentrification in a positive light.

Because residents establish East of the River as Black space, encouraging change that creates investment east of the river, then, is a means of further claiming racioeconomic agency for Anacostia. Dollars that were once spent west of the river and can now be spent east of the river become racialized, and demands for the ability to "spend that disposable income close to where [people] work" is a means of requesting, emphasizing, and reinforcing the continued importance of investment in, for, and by the Washington Black community.

These questions of investment and agency pervade the discussions of specific changes that the neighborhood is undergoing. There is an inherent problem in development that proceeds in the community without the input of the community, as is seen in the talk about the bait and switch of displacement or in development or even social services that happens primarily to benefit the (non) profiteers who provide the backing. What, then, could community investment in neighborhood change look like? The case study of the Bridge Park project, to which I turn next, provides both some answers and a few new questions.

## (Not) Building Bridges: Community Investment and Community Benefit

When I began this project in 2011, the Google Maps directions on my newly acquired iPhone led me on a twisted route down Ninth Street NW, onto the C Street Expressway (I-395 North) and a tangle of lanes where interstates 695 and 295 merged as they crossed the Anacostia River. Exiting in time to catch Exit 3A for Suitland Parkway/Anacostia involved crossing four lanes of hurried and none-too-kind traffic, and I always breathed a sigh of relief when I had made it safely onto Howard Road SE and up the shady streets toward my research sites.

This somewhat harrowing three-freeway trip was due to the reconstruction of the Eleventh Street bridge, the historic Anacostia river crossing that has existed in one form or another since approximately 1800.[17] Between 2009 and 2015 the bridge was completely rebuilt, expanding the number of lanes the bridge could carry in both directions and providing separate routes for travelers needing local exits versus those traveling toward I-95. This project made downtown Anacostia complicated to reach for several years. Ultimately the plan was to provide for easier flows of traffic across the river, and secondarily to enable a huge change to the face of the neighborhood: the building of Eleventh Street Bridge Park.

The Bridge Park project aims to use the pylons of the former bridge as an elevated park spanning the Anacostia River, linking the Ward 6 neighborhoods of Capitol Hill and Navy Yard to Anacostia. The website for the project features a computer-generated rendering of people watching an outdoor movie from chairs and boats, a dance performance taking place in an outdoor-seating venue, children playing in splash fountains, and people of all races sitting and talking at cafe tables and on riverside boardwalks.[18] It looks like any ad for any new high-end development, except that in multiple places on the website there is strong emphasis on engagement with the residents of the neighborhoods on both sides of the river in the planning and execution of the park.

Robert had recently been hired to work for the nonprofit organization responsible for building the bridge when I interviewed him in 2016. He described the project to me as

> a vision to have this park that could be used for recreational purposes, that would be able to connect both Ward 8 and Ward 6 to one another. And so for a long time the Anacostia River has been seen as this divider, and so this could be used as a– a unifying, um, point. And so, one of the first things they did was actually go into the community and ask the community, is this something that the community wants. And so resoundingly, the answer was yes. And so, literally the project has always been community focused and community driven. And so they were very very intentional with engaging with the community, and in stakeholders in the community in terms of what the design looks like.

Robert's emphasis on the bridge park as being for the community is evident as he explains the process, describing how the group planning the park went to the community and asked for feedback. It is equally evident in the fact that he chooses to use the full form *community* three times in this stretch, even when he could have chosen to use a pronoun: imagine "one of the first things they did was to go into the community and ask them, is this something they want." The choice to repeat *community* three times underscores the importance of the community aspect of the project, which he goes on to elaborate:

> We want this park to be completely owned um and– and the direction of it to come from the community. And so the way that they were engaging with the community, I mean, honestly I think it's going to change the way or it should change the way that development takes place in the city. Especially in communities

that have been neglected or disadvantaged communities. I think it s– it could definitely serve as a model for how development can come where, um, the community can, um, become a part of the development as opposed to they're just getting told what's gonna happen ya know once a decision has already been made.

Robert contrasts the Bridge Park development with the ways that he perceives that "development takes place in the city," particularly in communities that have been neglected. He explains exactly what the other way looks like: "They're just getting told what's gonna happen once a decision has already been made." This changes the role of the community: that they are just the recipients of the change, whatever that change might be. This is exactly the opposite of the kind of process Robert describes in the first excerpt, where *community* appears seven times in a short stretch of speech. Instead of a process that is "community focused and community driven," these other types of development models are top-down and may not ultimately serve the community they aim to serve.

For many of my interviewees the Bridge Park project represents community investment. The project is physically headquartered at the Town Hall Education Arts and Recreation Campus, or THEARC, located at the border of Wards 7 and 8. THEARC, which opened in 2005, is a $27 million facility that houses a Boys and Girls Club chapter, a teaching arm of the Washington City Ballet, the upper division of the Washington School for Girls, the Phillips Collection art museum, DC Central Kitchen, and several neighborhood-planning coalitions.[19] THEARC further has recreation and arts facilities, a community garden, and a health center, all of which exist to both serve the communities east of the river and enrich opportunities made available to them.[20]

In my conversations with Anacostia community residents, many brought up THEARC as an instance of investment in the area that meets the needs of residents. Part of this may be how it is situated and the presence of organizations that have a clear utility in the community: the Boys and Girls Club provides a safe place for children to be when their parents are at work; Covenant House houses and helps homeless young adults; and the Washington Children's Hospital provides needed medical help across the river from all the major area hospitals.

When it comes to Bridge Park, however, some feel that its utility is less clear. "Who cares about a bridge?" ANC commissioner Tracey asks me.

> Like, that's just not what we're thinking about right now. Like I told [a reporter] I said, 'I get it. I understand that that could have an impact on our community in five years.' I said, 'But guess what? Like, we gotta keep everybody alive this year. As an ANC commissioner, no one's coming to me right now on that's [not having a park] their devastating thing. Like, people are getting evicted! I was on a panel for community-housing trust, um, a few weeks ago, and I said you know I drive up my street some Saturdays at the beginning of the month and I see people's furniture on the sidewalk. People are getting evicted. They don't care about this bridge. Like their– they have no clue that this bridge is coming because they're trying to make sure they have somewhere to live month to month. That's people's concern.

Tracey contrasts the idea of Bridge Park with the reality of eviction in order to position her take on the park. She evokes the very vivid image of eviction: "I drive up my street some Saturdays at the beginning of the month and I see people's furniture on the sidewalk." By providing this very clear image she is able to make her listener, who in this case is twofold—both the reporter to whom she originally gave this opinion and, in her retelling, to me as the interviewer—focus on the harm done to residents of the community. This then brings in sharp contrast the fact that these people "don't care about this bridge . . . they're trying to make sure they have somewhere to live."

Setting up this contrast also allows Tracey to be both in favor of and against Bridge Park. By framing her discussion in terms of the needs of her constituents she is able to criticize overly optimistic views about whom the park will serve, emphasizing that it does not meet the needs of her constituents, whose concerns are much more immediate. At the same time, it allows her *not* to say "the Bridge Park is a bad idea" or indicate that she thinks it is a waste of money. She is able to carefully take a stance that Bridge Park is not the best use of resources at this time without directly opposing its construction.

Tracey's careful stance-taking here is in line with how other residents talk about the trade-offs between development and services. Especially for middle-class residents like Robert, Tracey, and Justin, the idea that any development in the community *must* serve the community is paramount in how they discuss that development. Justin, for instance, adds,

I do welcome the– a lot of the growth and expansion of the . . . the building you know the what's coming in, um, again I just don't think that it has to be a trade-off in terms of access. If– if you're building new centers, and if you're building . . . I don't think it it it means that, "Okay now that this is here," it has to be, um, uh, something that folks here can't participate in or that's restricted because of cost or or whatever. I also think that, again what I said, the ki– the kind of statements of things that that progress makes, um, a lot of the communities that have been allowed to just kind of deteriorate, deteriorate, deteriorate and then you come in and you build these new megastructures et cetera. And it says to me, these are things that could've happened a long time ago, and it could've happened in a way such that, um, people who were here benefited from it and they didn't have to be displaced. So, um,

and that's kind of the the, um, that the– the– the I guess the the–
di– dichotomy or the kind of mix or in that is that you let things
deteriorate, people move out, and then our people get displaced
and then you build all of these marvelous new things that you
know that could have been there.

Like Tracey, Justin takes a measured approach to discussing development and who it should serve. "I don't think [development]
means that . . . it has to be . . . something folks here can't participate in or that's restricted because of cost," he says. This statement
presupposes that at least some development has taken exactly this
position: that "people here" (residents of Anacostia) can't benefit from the development that is taking place. At the same time,
Justin goes a step further, assigning agency to the developers.
He explains how things here have been deteriorating, which he
emphasizes through repetition, but then things do get built. That
these buildings can exist, and thrive, in the community he takes
as evidence that the building "could've happened long ago" and it
could have benefited the community. Instead, he sees a nefarious
cycle whereby the exclusion of Anacostia from development that
would best serve its residents is not out of some sort of benign
neglect but is instead a carefully orchestrated project: the community is allowed to deteriorate so that investors feel justified in
both not serving the community and later building new things to
bring new people in.

Bridges are fundamentally connectors—ways to help people
cross bodies of water or other features they otherwise cannot. But
they can be created to be only one-way. The ways that Anacostians talk about development in their neighborhood is important
because it implicitly resists a common narrative used to justify development policies that displace existing residents. Inclusion of
community in development reframes development as being for
the people in the community, asserting, "We do not want help on
your terms, we want it on ours." For Anacostians, a bridge needs to

connect them to Washington, not the other way around: it needs to enhance Black space, not become a means for white people to encroach on it.

### Conclusion: "Better for Who?"

The stopping of the Space Finding Tour bus is momentous and important in understanding the economic flows that might privilege outside investors, especially those who are, as Kiesha puts it, "of other ethnic groups." The action of stopping the bus, preventing it from moving through the community, is a visible means of claiming control over the physical space. This claiming takes place linguistically as well: residents reject notions that any change that results in displacement or that otherwise doesn't benefit them is actually a form of "help." This rejection takes place linguistically as well, through the cognitive metaphor that calling the bus a "safari" evokes to begin with.

Conceptual metaphor is a pervasive discourse strategy that many linguists, most prominently George Lakoff, have examined.[21] In conceptual metaphor, multiple levels of connections are made between a source domain and a target domain, wherein the target domain comes to be talked about in terms of the source domain. For example, we often use the metaphor TIME IS MONEY when we talk about "saving time," "investing our time," or whether or not someone else can "spare" some of their time for us. The operations of these aspects of the metaphor are often below the level of conscious awareness; they become part of our discourse without our noticing their connection and become part of the ways in which we make sense of our world.

The conceptual metaphor created for the bus ride, DEVELOPMENT IS A SAFARI, works to connect several smaller comparisons in a way that allows the community to reject the seemingly benign benevolence of a "space-finding tour." Those on a hood safari are on a vehicle being driven through an area, so this part of the metaphor is quite literal. Developers board a bus and cross the river, then have the important parts of their journey pointed out by a guide. The fact that this activity is based on a vehicle tour makes the term *safari* appropriate, and it is the aspects of who is involved in a safari that make this metaphor so useful for the residents of Anacostia.

In a wild animal safari the people on the safari are insulated from any contact with animals on the safari, as though they are at a zoo. They are coming to peer in but not to touch. The use of the term *safari* therefore points out the degree to which the developers are distanced from the residents of the neighborhood. They are there to be driven around, to have the amazing features pointed out to them, but they are not getting off the bus to engage with the animals. You don't get to pet a lion on a safari—you just go to view its habitat and perhaps take a photo using a long-range lens. The use of *safari*, therefore, emphasizes the degree to which the developers are separate from the community. Ostensibly, they are there to spur economic development, but *safari* by itself does the work of showing that the viewers are there just to tour and, not coincidentally, to remain separate from those whose community they are coming to help grow.

The second relevant aspect of a safari is the question of who benefits from it. A safari doesn't exist to help the animals, and in fact for a large number of safaris, the point is to hunt. Even in a benign sightseeing safari the people who gain from the safari are the people on the safari, who get views and photos, and their guides. Kevin points this out when he says, "You know, money changes hands, but you know, the exotic animals never see any of that stuff." The safari metaphor suggests that the residents of Anacostia are not going to benefit from the developers on their bus.

The most problematic aspect of this metaphor is what people on a safari go to see. The reason that safari participants are asked to sit calmly inside their vehicle, of course, is because the animals they have come to see are dangerous. The idea of developers coming on a safari, then, implies that the people in Anacostia are exotic, and wild, and dangerous—exactly the reputation that the neighborhood has among the rest of the city and which its residents work hard to combat (to say nothing, of course, of the implication that the residents are animals, which reflects centuries of racist attitudes toward people of African descent).

Importantly, however, this positioning all happens via the use of *hood safari* by the residents themselves, not by the developers. Coming from the residents themselves, "hood safari" does the work of connecting the three things: that developers are there not to interact, that it is the developers who will benefit, and that the residents will not benefit from anything the developers choose to do. By renaming the space-finding tours as hood safaris, the residents of Anacostia recharacterize the people who are on them as greedy hunters. They underscore the degree to which development is not intended to help them and the degree to which the developers are insulated from the neighborhood and its people. Ultimately, by characterizing the developers as hunters who are not there to benefit the community, they resist the characterization of themselves as animals as well—rejecting the narrative that Anacostia is a place of danger and wildness.

I have shown how race is mapped onto the physical geography of Washington and how this racialized geography characterizes East of the River as proudly Black space. The insistence on the value of Black space serves to counter claims developers might make. Black space becomes a means of highlighting Black success and reframes the east-of-the-river communities as places of culture with money to spend. This reframing is not unlike the reframing of newcomers as white (see chapter 1). As evidenced by the kinds of services provided by the library, there is great socioeconomic disadvantage in Anacostia. The understanding that Anacostia is home to residents with money to burn and nowhere to burn it takes aim at outsiders' willingness to encroach on the space. It claims the space for the people who already live there, demanding that amenities be brought to them and for them. Claiming an African American identity for the space means claiming agency: demanding that development proceed with and for the community, not to "save" it. When Empower D.C. objected to the space-finding tour, their representative said, "The city and developers believe the community could be 'better' with more development, restaurants, higher income people. It is our job to ask: Better for who?"[22]

Residents of Anacostia and its East of the River neighbors answer that question when they intersect the racial geography with their own development, plans, and desires. For Anacostians, to talk about their neighborhood is to racialize it. Refracting the racialized geography of Washington, DC, onto their neighborhood turns their neighborhood into Black space. If we begin by seeing the neighborhood as Black space, the process of gentrification itself becomes racialized, discourses that create negative links between African Americans and social statuses are rejected, and African Americanness is linked to the neighborhood through language itself. Racializing the neighborhood opens the door for the assertion of the importance of development that supports the Black success already inherent in the neighborhood. "Better for who?" asks Empower D.C. It must be better for us, Anacostia answers, and in the clarifying words of Gus, "Us, meaning Black folk."

## Notes

1. Drew Hansen, "Police Arrest 1 during Protest of Bus Tour of Anacostia River Development," *Washington Business Journal*, April 19, 2016.

2. Hansen, "Police Arrest 1."

3. The crossover point, according to estimates from the US Census, seems to be approximately 2015, when of DC's then 602,000 residents, 301,000 identified as "Black or African American."

4. Irvine and Gal, "Language Ideology"; Modan, *Turf Wars*. See Irvine and Gal for the definition and Modan for a DC-specific application of this theory.

5. One very instructive example of this is the massive backlash experienced by the editor of the popular DC blog *PoPville*. "PoP" originally stood

for "Prince of Petworth," a self-moniker assumed by Dan Silverman, a white man who took up residence in Petworth, an east-of-the-park neighborhood, in 2006. He chronicled DC's changes and began to raise his family, then in 2016 chose to move to Van Ness, a west-of-the-park neighborhood, in search of better schools. He was met with the derision of many of his longtime readers.

6. District of Columbia, *Inclusionary Zoning*.

7. Smithsonian Anacostia Community Museum, "Making of a Museum."

8. The Francis pool in West End DC, a predominately African American part of downtown DC immediately east of Georgetown.

9. There is no currently named Stewart Road SE. It is possible that Gus is referring to a renamed road, or making a speech error and referring to Stanton Road, which runs through Barry Farm.

10. Anacostia Library website.

11. City of Washington DC, "DC's Economic Strategy."

12. Michael Fletcher, "A Shattered Foundation: African Americans Who Bought Homes in Prince George's Have Watched Their Wealth Vanish," *Washington Post*, January 24, 2015.

13. Emily Wax, "Gentrification Covers Black and White Middle-Class Home Buyers in the District," *Washington Post*, July 29, 2011.

14. The new offices of the Department of Homeland Security in the former St. Elizabeth's Hospital compound.

15. By the time we sat down for this interview, Tracey had left the DC schools and was working for an educational nonprofit.

16. JDLand.com, the Harlow/Square 769N.

17. Jaffe, *Dream City;* Smithsonian Anacostia Museum, *Black Washingtonians*.

18. Building Bridges Across the River website.

19. In 2014 the lower division of the school opened in the building formerly run by Our Lady of Perpetual Help, further solidifying the connection between the church as a figure of the local Black community and other organizations that exist to serve that community.

20. THEARC website.

21. Lakoff and Johnson, *Metaphors We Live By;* and Lakoff, *All New Don't Think*.

22. Hansen, "Police Arrest 1."

## Conclusion

# "It's Change"
### Bridging the River

On an unseasonably warm day in mid-March, toward the end of my fieldwork, I finish an interview and decide to treat myself to an afternoon of strolling at one of the crown jewels of Anacostia: Anacostia Riverfront Park. Nearly one hundred years old, the park flanks the eastern side of the Anacostia River and offers scenic vistas of the Navy Yard, Washington Nationals Park, and the rest of downtown Washington, DC.[1] After a short drive from my interviewee's house, I park my car and walk a mile along the river trail that stretches itself immediately beside the river, noticing the sunshine, the calm water of the Anacostia, and the cherry trees a few weeks before blossom.

Walking southwestward along the trail leads me to Frederick Douglass Memorial Bridge, the westernmost crossing over the Anacostia River. One of the busiest river crossings in the DC area, but deemed structurally deficient, the bridge is headed for renovation, just like the Eleventh Street bridge on the other side of the community. Renderings of the construction on the project's website show a decidedly contemporary design, with a wide roadway flanked by three graceful arches on each side that terminate on both sides of the river in miniature circular parks featuring traffic-controlling roundabouts. Plans tout a multiuse walkway to encourage cycling and pedestrian traffic, and esplanades appear beneath the bridge on both sides of the river. Like the plans for Eleventh Street Bridge Park, the renderings of Frederick Douglass

Bridge show happy families of all races walking along the esplanade, children skipping with balloons next to colorful murals, and people sitting and enjoying their view of the river.

On this day, however, the current bridge still stands, so I decide to experience the existing crossing. After a tiny wrong turn I find my way to the winding path that takes me from the park, up an embankment, to the narrow pedestrian walkway, which soars perilously over the river, flanked on my left by cars and trucks speeding their way into downtown DC. I am good with heights, but only when strapped safely into an amusement park ride, and so after a few glimpses down at the water I find it necessary to keep my gaze firmly on the end of the path as I continue across, trying to refrain from contemplating the distance of the drop from the walkway into the river.

The other end of the bridge drops me directly into the heart of Washington's current transformations. It terminates at Navy Yard, the area where an actual naval yard once stood and from where ships left DC to travel the Potomac waterway to the Chesapeake Bay. For most of the last decade Navy Yard has instead been one of the centers of DC's gentrification process, growing by leaps and bounds thanks to the Nationals' ballpark, which was built in 2006. As though to signify exactly how thoroughly different this rapidly gentrifying side of the river is from the place I'd just left, the bridge terminates in a lot that at first seems to be full of shipping containers but which upon further scrutiny displays signs advertising its function as a parking lot for food trucks at lunchtime.

A short walk past the ballpark puts me at a newly built seafood bar, whose extensive selection of craft beers seemed mission-driven to cater to the affluent professionals expected to frequent the ballpark and its surrounds. From the bar I look back across the river toward the park I've just left, with the existing Frederick Douglass Bridge soaring over the river to my right.

That the beginning of the research for this book was marked by the complete renovation of the easternmost bridge to Anacostia and the work's completion is marked by the opening of a renovated bridge at its westernmost side is not an insignificant fact. It is also not coincidental. The changes in the neighborhood both precipitate and are precipitated by these changes in access. As movement east of the river becomes easier, moving *to* East of the River becomes easier as well, and the claims that existing residents make on their neighborhood are increasingly likely to be challenged.

The ways that Anacostians use language to assert place identity, and the ways that this place identity is inextricably intertwined with race identity, remain paramount as the residents, city leaders, and others look to the future of this area east of the river. Understanding these linguistic practices of place in turn helps us understand the ways in which the urban landscape is changing for Black people and what Black people might do in asserting the right to the kinds of change that most benefit their existing communities.

This final chapter considers the implications of understanding the ways that Black people use language to claim place identity. I begin by looking at what happens when the connections between race and place and race and class are flipped, as the residents of Anacostia flip them. While many of the explanations for urban change rely on subtly racist connections between Blackness and poverty, connecting Blackness to place in a positive way affects the kinds of claims Black people can make on their space.

These claims, then, have implications for how we think about preserving these kinds of urban areas. When Black space is valuable space that will be fought for, the "solutions" that must be engaged in order to change the urban landscape are necessarily different. I explore through the lens of my interviewees' words whether gentrification without displacement is possible and who might potentially benefit from urban change were it imagined differently.

Finally, I explore what a study of language use by a Black community within a gentrifying locale has to tell sociolinguistics. For a field that has long privileged explanations that center minori-

tized communities, particularly Black urban communities, sociolinguistics has still generally taken an etic, one-feature-at-a-time
approach to understanding the effects of race and social class on
language. A study of a place like Anacostia, where Black identity
is centered in all the ways that the residents use language to lay
claim to their space, reveals how discourse practices and features
of the linguistic system function in the enactment of place identity
and individuals' relationship to a changing social order. Importantly, studying the linguistic practices of place reveals the ways
in which class, race, and place identities are intersectional: when
place is racialized, so too is class, and so too are the conflicts of
space that arise because of them.

### Gentrification Discourse as a Form of Colorblind Racism

One of the most remarkable aspects of the interviews presented
here is the degree to which the residents of Anacostia consistently
link their experience of Blackness with their presence in the community, the community's success, and the neighborhood's opposition to change. Residents regularly recast gentrification entirely in
racial terms, despite the fact that at the time the interviews were
collected very little change had actually occurred in the racial demographics of the neighborhood.

The Big-D Discourses that link race to urban change generally
do so in a negative way, presenting differences in property values as though these are neutral, aracial facts. Some of the work
in allied fields such as sociology and urban geography has shown
that explanations for gentrification that rely on appeals to things
like blight and low property values in effect act as a proxy for race
by ignoring the ways lower property values occur because of the
systems that result in Black people living in a place to begin with.
Mary Pattillo, in her work on Chicago's north side, has shown that
African Americans, particularly middle-class African Americans
in the midst of gentrification, often appeal to the same sorts of

arguments that link gentrification to property values, reinforcing the embedded racist narratives of urban change.

A possible explanation for the attractiveness of this kind of explanation lies in one of the frames of colorblind racism, as sociologist Eduardo Bonilla-Silva explains. The explanations for colorblind racism have their roots in critical race theory, the turn in race studies that came out of legal scholarship in the 1980s, was strengthened in the 1990s with work on intersectionality theory, and has continued to be at the forefront of social science work in the twenty-first century.

As Bonilla-Silva explains in his book *Racism without Racists*, colorblind racism is the ideology whites largely adopted following the civil rights era, which replaced overt ideas that Black people were inferior with a way of thinking that, by encouraging whites to minimize the "seeing" of racial differences, provided new, more covert ways of expressing racist ideas.[2]

Bonilla-Silva explains four frames through which whites interpret racism and in turn erase the effects of racism through their explanations. Cultural racism is the idea that people are responsible for their own situations due to differences in cultural values. Naturalism is the idea that racism is a part of the human fabric and that some, or many, of its facets simply cannot be avoided due to human nature. Abstract liberalism is the idea that economic and political liberalism are available to everyone; that is, everyone has equal opportunity and unequal results are due to some differences in how opportunities are or are not taken advantage of. Minimization is the idea that white people often deny accusations of racism, or attempt to explain to people of color that they are overemphasizing race or seeing a racial effect where there is none, when they argue against the effects of racism.

Most of these frames are active in the ways that gentrification is often talked about, particularly cultural racism and abstract liberalism. We might revisit comments from Justin here:

I also think that, um, again what I said, the ki– the kind of statements of things that that progress makes, um, a lot of the communities that have been allowed to just kind of deteriorate, deteriorate, deteriorate and then you come in and you build these new megastructures et cetera. And it says to me, these are things that could've happened a long time ago, and it could've happened in a way such that, um, people who were here benefited from it and they didn't have to be displaced.

Justin's quote flips on its head the narrative that the city is investing in Anacostia and repositions the neighborhood with respect to outside investment. The city's narrative, at least as Justin presents it, relies on an abstract liberalism appeal. There exists a place in the city in need of help, so it makes economic and social sense to invest in that area. However, Justin points out that this explanation obscures the way the city has allowed the area to fall into what he sees as disrepair. In his explanation the economic opportunities of Anacostia are prioritized above those of the city, and the city is complicit in the neighborhood's loss of amenities in the first place. Instead of an appeal to the abstraction of "investment," in Justin's telling the city becomes the driver of the "deterioration" of the buildings through its lack of investment; the city's willingness to step in to fix things now becomes the solution to a problem the city created for the express purpose of solving it later.

What Justin does not explicitly say here, however, is that the reason for this is the future likelihood of white residents moving in. This goes unstated in part because it is implicitly stated in the ways in which the residents talk about the neighborhood. The deictic juxtaposition of the Black "us" and the white "them," the reframing of whiteness in the neighborhood, the use of African American Language to talk about the ways the neighborhood is changing—these all contribute to centering race in the discussion of the changes taking place. As a result, there is resistance to the sort of abstract liberalism argument that sees gentrification as merely the logical outcome of the investment of money across the city. Changing the Big-D Discourses about gentrification in Anacostia from an economic discourse to a racial discourse in turn changes the relationship between race and change seen elsewhere. Rather than accepting the narrative that gentrification is primarily a matter of money, in Anacostia it becomes exclusively about race.

In the language of the interviewees, that Anacostia is Black space is not the inevitable *result* of demographic trends and in- and out-migration. If the existence of a large African American population in Anacostia is linked to lower property values, that link is the *effect* of deliberate neglect on the part of the city, not an incidental fallout of where people just happened to settle.

Instead of making the implicit link between race and place that winds up allowing race to proxy negatively for bad property values, blight, and crime—and in turn to justify change to the urban landscape that inevitably leads to change in racial demographics—residents' centering of Anacostia's Blackness in the ways they talk about their neighborhood changes the narrative. The link between race and place becomes explicit; the link between race and place becomes one to be exploited, not to justify gentrification but to justify viewing the neighborhood as one of the city's main assets. I turn to this next.

### Reversing the Race/Space Proxy

In his 2010 book, *Disintegration*, Pulitzer Prize–winning author, *Washington Post* columnist, and DC resident Eugene Robinson argues that what is conventionally understood as the American Black community is in fact four different communities, differentiated by access to wealth and power and by their relationship to the American descendants of slaves (who make up the majority of Black people of color in the United States).[3] He argues that treating all Black people of color as one group may have served political expediency in the past, and he points to the power of groups such as the NAACP. But Robinson also argues that in a post–civil rights era age, during a time that a Black president governed the United States, this ignoring of difference between kinds of Black identities has the effect of hindering the growth that otherwise might take place for Black communities.[4]

This tendency to interpret all Black people as a monolithic group with the same interests has a long history in American thought, stretching back to the days of one-drop rules that declared that a person with any African ancestry was subject to discriminatory laws. Work in Black geography and Black sociology argues that racial identity is the chief predictor of how African American people relate to, and are related to, American culture. While segregation may no longer be legal, most Americans still live surrounded mostly by people who look like them.[5] Space is still understood as racially constructed—especially in Washington, DC. Because of this, looking at the ways in which Anacostians talk about their space, especially as that space experiences demographic and economic shifts, has implications for how we think about the connections between race and place broadly and how we enfranchise Black people and other people of color in their own changing communities.

First, it is helpful to affirm that metaphors and narratives about gentrification and change are usually little more than thinly veiled references to race. Certainly it is often true that the areas inhabited disproportionately by people of color are significantly more likely to have lower property values than those inhabited by whites. But to imagine that this is an accident, rather than the result of centuries of official policies and unofficial social practice, is to ignore the racialized underpinnings of the American economy.[6] Yet studies from the neighboring fields of sociology and anthropology show that developers and incoming white residents who benefit from the changes being made to an area buy into (both metaphorically and actually) these racist narratives about gentrification—as do the people of color who may be displaced.

Pattillo, for example, in her work on the Lakefront neighborhood of Chicago and the debate about whether to remove a major public housing development that occupied newly prime real estate on the shores of Lake Michigan, shows how the debate over this community was limited to discussions of the correct number of units and the definition of low-income housing while at the same time ignoring the racial underpinnings of who would be moved.[7] No one, including the mostly African American community living inside the public housing buildings, was permitted to frame the debate in terms of race. Similarly, within Washington, DC, specifically, Prince's work shows how debates about gentrification translate into debates about race, and Modan's analysis of the use of *filth* in discussions of a grant proposal for public toilets is best read as a coded reference to the Salvadorans in the neighborhood of Mount Pleasant.[8] Each of these examples shows the way a racialized logic of the debates about neighborhood change becomes obscured.

In the subjects of these works, the racializing of the neighborhood is often done by those who are outside the place under discussion and then are often taken up by those whom it affects. In the interviews here, however, I show how Anacostia residents racialize their neighborhood differently than outsiders do, though both outsiders and insiders view the neighborhood as Black. This racializing happens at every linguistic level of language and through a variety of strategies: through deictic positioning (see chapter 1), through the use of African American English morphosyntax (chapter 3), and through the discussion of racialized geography (chapter 4). Such racializing changes the social meaning of the neighborhood as Black space; instead, it racializes the process of gentrification and rejects a narrative that positions Anacostia as dirty, dangerous, and poor but it does so in a way that reevaluates

Blackness as the most positive aspect of this space (see chapter 2). Foregrounding Anacostia as Black space turns it into Black *place,* as in the work of Scollon and Scollon.[9] By discursively racializing Anacostia the interviewees stake their claim on it, imbuing it with the meaning of "for us."

Making Anacostia into Black place reimagines what Black places are and why they matter. It turns the racial segregation of the neighborhood from a liability into its most important asset: it is here that DC's Black community has maintained its roots and here that outsiders, like newcomer-turned-neighborhood commissioner Tracey, find their people and their culture. These aspects make Anacostia worth protecting: it is a beautiful space, valuable space, safe space, and owned space. In this way of speaking the link between race and place remains unbroken, but it proxies entirely differently. Instead of being the implicit reason the neighborhood is ripe for the taking, Blackness becomes the explicit reason the neighborhood is valuable as it is, and thus becomes the cornerstone for claims of agency in the changes that will occur.

This reversal has broader implications for how we think about the connections made to other Black spaces across the United States. The interviewees here suggest a way forward into reversing the narrative of the monolithic Black American community. This is in line with recent projects in allied fields such as Chocolate Cities Sociology, Black Cultural Geography, and the 1619 Project, which takes the view that West Africans brought by the transatlantic slave trade, not European religious dissidents, should be considered the true founders of the United States of America. Such reversals of the racial narrative of the United States experience change in who owns these narratives: they make US culture into a culture that is Black-owned, and they demand Blacks' rights to tell a story about the country that centers Black culture. Like the discussions of Anacostia, these reversals change the agency: who gets to make a claim on culture, on the country, and on where they live.

Such recentering further points the way forward on how those who are concerned about changing the nature of rapid urban growth and displacement ought to go about it. When we take as a given residents' own agency and make visible the connections between race and place that usually proxy as a means for taking space from people of color, it changes the nature of non-Black outsiders' understanding of the space. As the residents who responded to the "hood safari" put it, "This is not space: This is a community." Understanding the ways these race-space connections are made, and the ways by which residents of a Black neighborhood can reverse them, opens the door for urban planners, community leaders, and those who might genuinely wish to invest in the neighborhood in a way that supports it and can privilege this understanding of community by making primary the residents' claims on the space.

**Chocolate Place, Chocolate Power**

On any sunny day in Washington it's easy to see why people remained in Hillsdale. Driving down streets named for trees, it's simple to focus on the quaintness of the rows of townhouses tucked between trees with wide grassy embankments in front of them. I find, as I park and walk around the neighborhood, that with my head full of all I've learned from my interviews, it's hard to view the Barry Farm public housing project as a dilapidated mess that investors and outsiders typically paint it as. It is easy to instead imagine Tana and her brother attending nursery school here forty years ago under the mature shade trees or refusing their mother's attempts to get them out of the pool at the recreation center.

On this day in 2017 about half the townhomes are boarded up and several of the buildings are in the process of being reduced to rubble by large yellow backhoes. The brick red paint delineating the doorway of each home is peeling, and most buildings' roof shingles are discolored and in need of replacement. Yet something about the neighborhood still feels bucolic, as though it might easily be a higher-rent community designed not for people in need of economical housing but for Washington's elite suburbanites. Seated at the bottom of Fort Stanton Hill, the buildings obscure any views of the Capitol dome and the Washington Monument, making it easy to forget the teeming, busy metropolis that lies just across the river. It's a conflicting feeling that encapsulates my position as a researcher, with one foot firmly rooted in the stories of my informants—in their histories and their love for this place—and the other foot standing strong in understanding the economic flows that make this land desirable.

Barry Farm features prominently in this book for good reason. In the same way that Georgetown is metonymic for gentrification and for the takeover of Black space by whites, Barry Farm is metonymic for exactly the opposite: a place that is unabashedly Black and where Black community must be protected. Barry Farm stands for everything good and everything bad about the Southeast Quadrant, all at once: here crime is slightly higher and the average income is lower than in other parts of the neighborhood, while at the same time the trees and the grass and the very orientation of the buildings as rows of two-story homes instead of a big brick apartment building lend a feel of hominess and intimacy incongruent with a standard schema for a public housing project.

The new structure to be built will provide more units than the existing project does, including some public housing, some income-based affordable-housing, and some housing to be offered at market rates. But current Barry Farm residents will have to move elsewhere, at least temporarily, and there won't be enough affordable units for all to return. This has understandably caused residents of the neighborhood to decry a bait and switch trick by the city, to say nothing of the fact that statistics show that lower-income residents who are displaced for any reason often lack the ability to return.

Prince, in her work on gentrification patterns in Washington, DC, charts how the flows throughout the city have meant a concentration of African American people east of the river as middle-income African Americans, priced out of Northwest Quadrant neighborhoods, have slowly concentrated in Anacostia and its surrounds. At the same time she points out that conceiving of Washington, DC, as a Chocolate City changes how people conceive of Black power. Many of her interviewees made claims that Washington was "99.5 percent Black," thus codifying Washington in terms of racial geography (and just as my interviewees did, as discussed in chapter 4). One way to see this concentration is as a concentration of poorer people, those "most disadvantaged and least able to fight back," as Prince puts it.[10] However, I suggest that another way to view this is as a concentration of Black power.

Anacostia has leveraged this power into a variety of community-driven resources. Drawing on the strong history of places such as the Anacostia Community Museum and Black-centered churches such as Our Lady of Perpetual Help, outreach efforts to Black neighbors within the neighborhood have been a continuing tradition. The decade preceding the work for this book saw the creation of new Anacostia organizations such as the nonprofit Far Southeast Family Strengthening Collaborative (FSFSC), which, aside from providing support to young families through economic opportunity and civic engagement, offers parenting classes, advice for enrolling in public programs and direct service programs, as well as giving out local small grants, operating work programs for middle and high schoolers, and finding jobs for recent graduates.

The Town Hall Education Arts and Recreation Campus sits on 16.5 acres just east of Anacostia proper. It houses several youth, arts, and social service organizations, a theater for events and local productions, and a farm where children and adults can learn sustainable, local agricultural methods. Its parent organization, Building Bridges Across the River, oversees THEARC, the Eleventh Street bridge project, the large farm on the main campus and smaller plots throughout the community, and a workforce development center. As it is within a short walk of a metro station, the campus is accessible and usable even by those with limited transportation means.

Organizations like FSFSC and THEARC reflect the shift in Anacostia's self-image from a concentration of Black residents (meaning a concentration of people who are least able to fight back) to a concentration of Black people with agency. These sorts of organizations, coupled with already existing organizations like the ACM, mean that the community can drive its own growth and change and define its support in a way that privileges the hyperlocal perspective and empowers the residents to make change for themselves. They change the landscape of the neighborhood precisely because they *don't* change the landscape of the neighborhood: it becomes impossible to displace these organizations, and therefore becomes more difficult to displace those who are a part of them. Middle-class African American residents who are involved with these organizations think of them and frame them as the way by which the community empowers itself, for example, when Robert describes the Bridge Park project as creating a "unifying point" or Porter sees new incomers as an "opportunity to grow." Similarly, Tracey, in her position as neighborhood commissioner, offers a counternarrative to the narrative of displacement:

> I hesitate to scream and shout gentrification and pushing out
> and all of those things. Because I actually do know a few seniors
> who've passed and their children have decided to sell their homes.
> And my advice is just, you know, if you're gonna sell it make sure
> you get, you know—make sure you're not selling your parents'
> home for pennies and then somebody's coming in and gutting it
> and refurbishing it and selling it for three times what you got for it.

Tracey expresses her concern about homes being sold and then flipped.[11] Most of the time flipping also involves making improvements to a home and adding trendy interior finishes. It is often seen as an indicator of gentrification taking place, and data scientists use the percentage of flipped homes in overall sales as a gentrification indicator.[12] Tracey is concerned about making sure that the original owners get their money's worth out of the deal ("not selling for pennies"), not about the flipping itself. In her telling the desire to sell is reasonable and understandable and does not constitute "pushing out." Instead, it is part of a process that can benefit residents—she just wants to make sure that it does.

Tana, who volunteers with the ACM, similarly rejects the idea of gentrification as a concept, instead choosing to focus on the ways that neighborhood change benefits her own community:

> Well I don't own the neighborhood. And everything changes. Everything changes. And unfortunately it took me until I was in my forties to realize that everything changes, and if you don't change with it and stay current you'll get left behind. You'll be left behind. You'll be a dinosaur, a relic, you know, and I think I just think that that the times are just too interesting to allow that to happen to someone, so I had to you know just finally embrace the idea that my neighborhood is going to change, you know. My neighborhood is going to change. There will be people who perhaps had lived here at one time who won't be able to afford to live here. That I don't like, I still don't like, but that's not the problem of the people who are moving in. They don't have– they really don't have anything to do with that, you know, and everybody needs a place to live. So I don't even use the– You notice I didn't use the G word. I didn't use it. I don't use it. I don't use it. Because when you use that word it feels negative. You say the word "gentrification" and it translates into these people are being pushed out by these other people whoever the others are, they're pushing them out, and it's unfair, and it's racist, and it's this and it's that, and it's, um, class warfare it's all of these different things. I didn't use it. It's change.

In Tana's talk the word *gentrification* becomes neutral. It becomes "change." Like Tracey, she distances herself from the idea of gentrification as displacement. Through comments like "you'll be a dinosaur," she evaluates the idea of stagnation, not the idea of change, as being the problem.

There is a logical coupling between the existence of these community organizations and the ways that those involved with them talk about the neighborhood's change. Within these places, change is driven *by* the community *for* the community. Placing value on the kinds of narratives and discourses the community members use makes change a process in which residents are invested and valued alongside developers. Understanding the ways in which people use language—their stories, their framings, and the language structure itself—to stake claims on their community points a way forward to valuing the community and its own desires. It serves the same purpose as a place like THEARC does: making a concentration of Black people into a place of strength.

### Taking a Raciolinguistic Approach to Place

The study of sociolinguistics has always been rooted in the study of place, and no small number of foundational sociolinguistic studies have been rooted in *this* particular place. Washington, DC, has long been an important location in the sociolinguistic imagination: neither cleanly South nor North and with a demographic history that privileged people of color, especially throughout the immediate post–civil rights era.[13] It has served as a location for linguists to learn about the language of African American people since the field's inception.

The study of African American Language has long been plagued with what Wolfram defines as the myth of aregionality.[14] Because the field is based in the dialect mapping studies of the early twentieth century, linguists have long thought they had identified a language variety that existed in similar form across the United States.[15] Even though the foundational studies that underpinned sociolinguistic exploration of AAL themselves showed the effects of regional variation within the variety, the assumption of aregionality led to decades of privileging research on AAL.[16] At the same time, regional work about AAL remains relatively abundant: we know about regional AAL in the Susquehanna Valley of Pennsylvania,[17] in California,[18] in Texas,[19] in Iowa and Tennessee,[20] and of course in the eastern urban cities of New York[21] and Washington.[22] Recently, the launch of the Corpus of Regional African American Language has made accessible the study of regional variation within AAL.[23] The corpus, which aims to gather AAL data from across the United States in comparable datasets, makes possible the close examination of language in ways that will allow explorations of the effect of place while controlling for other social factors.

Linguists have long been aware that place identity is something done through language. Dialect mapping, language judgment mapping, and the ever-popular dialect quizzes all rely on the understanding that speakers are likely to perform their connections to place identity using their language.[24] This language is even further connected to place identity through the fact that it becomes stereotyped and commodified.

Recently, the field of raciolinguistics has recognized that, as linguistic anthropologist Jonathan Rosa describes it, the "conaturalization of language and race is a key feature of modern governance, such that languages are perceived as racially embodied and race is perceived as linguistically intelligible."[25] In other words, those who work in this field perceive that the connections between language and race are not easily disentangled and, in fact, work in tandem at a level invisible to the average speaker. Linguists have also exploited this connection, especially early on when they simply assumed African American Language was what one heard when interviewing every African American, especially working-class males.

The raciolinguistic approach suggests that rather than language patterns being the result of someone's racioethnic identity or their affiliation/association with other people who share that identity, race is something that is "put on through language" in particular ways, much like any other kind of language identity. A raciolinguistic approach assumes that language use facilitates and normalizes the construction of racial identity.

What this book shows is that racial identity co-occurs with other kinds of identity, particularly identities of place and class. It also shows that while racial identity is accomplished in part through the use of readily identifiable elements of the linguistic system, such as phonology and morphosyntax, it is also accomplished through discourse. Racial identity is not only inseparable from language; it is also inseparable from these co-occurring identities and, in fact, is implicated in the construction of all of them.

This book also illustrates a final aspect of a more contemporary approach to language and race, namely, the inextricability of multiple marginalized identities. The theoretical framework of intersectionality, as legal scholar Kimberlé Crenshaw first developed it, argues that multiple aspects of social and political identity combine to create unique forms of discrimination that are particular not to any single identity but to the combination of identities.[26] Thus, for instance, a Black woman might face workplace discrimination that is not specifically due to gender, if the company does not discriminate against white women, and not specifically due to race, if the company does not discriminate against Black men. Similarly, advocacy designed to ameliorate discrimination based on one marginalized identity may fail to address the needs of people with multiple identities, such as when feminist movements fail to acknowledge the contribution of race to discrimination against Black women and end up serving mostly white women.

In Anacostia the largest intersection exists between race and class. Concerns related to the influx of middle-class residents—mostly African American, during the course of this study, but increasingly white as the years move forward—drive a great deal of the ways people in the neighborhood frame their discussions of what is going on. The ability of a working-class Black neighborhood to create economic growth change while also maintaining the neighborhood's sense of community for the people who live there is fraught with potential conflicts. New amenities mean restaurants and parks for residents, but they also can drive growth of a population whose demographics don't match those of the existing neighborhood.

In her work in Chicago, Pattillo identifies the importance of the middle-class "middlemen" in the process of gentrification.[27] Middle-class African Americans, she argues, serve an important role as advocates, provided they do not themselves perpetuate economic arguments for gentrification that hide its racist effects. The discourses in this study show similar aspects of this kind of middle-class advocacy and point to a way it might work best.

Reframing gentrification processes in terms of race in all the ways the neighborhood residents in this study do is a way of re-coupling the neighborhood's Black identity with its working-class identity. Making Black Washingtonians "our people" means articulating that change has to help all residents. It is not enough, they argue, for the city to make and suggest changes based on income disparities in the guise of "helping" lower-income residents. In emphasizing the Black character of the neighborhood, residents implicitly define to whom agency is granted, reclaiming their neighborhood for themselves. By studying language in a place where racial identity is relatively constant but where class identities are in flux, it becomes possible to see the ways in which racialized language does the work of claiming identities of place.

### The Last Bastion: Holding Out and Holding Up

In this book I have explored the ways in which residents of Anacostia consider, and reconsider, the nature of the change in their neighborhood. I've looked at how gentrification itself becomes reduced to a racial issue, how residents position themselves in the face of neighborhood change, how African American Language does the work of instantiating Black local identity, and how this turns into neighborhood-based agency. As the residents are talking, however, the invisible hand of demographic change continues its sweep, ticking ever closer. Anacostia seems to be the last place that the forces of change that swept Georgetown and U Street almost half a century ago seem destined to come.

"Southeast– and I say Southeast because it most, uh, reflects what was left of what the community used to be like ethnically and also in terms of cultural– culturally. It seems like Ward 8 or southeast Anacostia is like the last, uh, bastion of the African American community," says Justin. *Bastion* is an unusual word, and perhaps all the more unusual to hear being used to describe a neighborhood. Yet Justin isn't the only one who uses this kind of language. Community organizer Thomas, in talking about the ways the neighborhood has changed, offers a similar perspective: "[Anacostia] is the last frontier in terms of affordability. This is it. It has it has older housing stock, and you know they don't have the class A apartments and those types of things, so. You going to find lower rents. And, you know, if– if you want to stay in the city, you don't have a lot of income, this is where people have moved to."

The invocation of words like *bastion* and *frontier* evokes a cognitive metaphor that compares gentrification to a war.[28] Bastion is an interesting word selection, for multiple reasons. One is that Anacostia is a literal bastion: Fort Stanton Hill, where Our Lady of Perpetual Help Church sits, not far from the Anacostia Community Museum, was a Civil War battlement erected to oversee the various military operations in Washington City.[29] But it is no longer the Union that must be held together. Instead, it is what Black residents feel is slowly being pushed aside: the people who look like them and, with the people, the root of Washington, DC itself. "We knew that once the subway was built Anacostia was going to change color," says Amy, the oldest interviewee in this book.

And it is. It's changing color. Because all of that area used to be–
People had their houses in their backyards backed up to Suitland
Parkway. And, um, they just, you know, people had to move out
a had to give up their– they had to give up their land and stuff
like that. Well at that time you know we all wanted to, uh, move
into better conditions and stuff like that so, we didn't think about
the value that these places are now. So genocide got in there and
worked. Took over.

Amy, who moved from her Barry Farm home in the mid-2000s to
live with her daughter in Northwest, makes a telling slip when she
talks about the racial shift in Anacostia. Reaching, presumably for
the word *gentrification,* she retrieves *genocide* instead, accidentally comparing the pushing out of the African American population to their extermination. While this is not happening in a literal
sense, the disappearance of Black Washingtonians from Anacostia
looks a great deal like a purposeful extermination.

The demographic data supports the idea that gentrification will
gain ground in Anacostia, as it shows growth accelerating rapidly
in the latter half of the 2010s. Between 2010 and 2017 the growth
of the number of white residents in the neighborhood accelerated
nearly fivefold (though the numbers were still so vanishingly small
that the total still constitutes fewer than two hundred white residents). Even during the years this research took place, the neighborhood changed dramatically. A bookstore opened. The first
standalone Starbucks opened. A branch of DC entrepreneur Andy
Shallal's restaurant chain, Busboys and Poets, opened. Historic
homes that lined Martin Luther King Boulevard were relocated to
another part of the neighborhood to make way for the Maple View
Flats Apartment Community, and after a multiyear fight, in spring
2019 boarded-up townhomes in Barry Farm began to be razed.

Southeast DC is the last frontier of change in Washington. As
bridges are rebuilt, it becomes ever easier to reach this area, with
its beauty and its affordable housing. So the residents talk of it

as the final place: the last bastion of DC's Black community, the last stronghold of the same Chocolate City culture that led Parliament-Funkadelic to write their famous song four decades ago. Community Museum employee Porter offers,

> Southeast is kind of the last bastion. It's starting to come over here now. We do see signs of it. But we have a place in that. We have a place in that whole process, right? We see gentrification as an opportunity for this neighborhood to grow. We're not looking at some of the negative things that people always say about gentrification, especially in this neighborhood. We want to be part of the change. We wanna be part of the change in a good way.

The linguistic practices that instantiate Anacostia, defining DC as Black space, in turn make it a place where Black voices matter. Black people stake a claim on the places that belong to them, the claim that Black people not only have a place in the land but, as Porter says, a place in the process. Listening to the practices of place points the way toward how these reframings, repositionings, and claim-stakings can empower people whose culture and place is encroached upon.

Rivers separated slave land from free land. Rivers served as the means for people to leave the Mississippi Delta for the North. Rivers determined where the seat of the US government would be. And, for a long time here, a river has divided "East" from "West," creating Black space for the people who've lived east of the river. This space has been upheld in how they talk about it—in their language they lay claim to a racialized space, emphasizing its history and its rootedness in Black community through the words themselves.

When Black people cross rivers it matters. In the near future there will be two new ways to cross the Anacostia River: from west to east but also from east to west. The connections will change and the experiences will change and the people will change.

If rivers are dividers, bridges are connectors, and the renovations of these two bridges are almost too apt a metaphor for the ways in which Anacostia seems poised to change. On the one hand, bridges allow Anacostians easy access to move toward downtown DC, toward the shops and places like the baseball stadium and the soccer stadium and all the restaurants around them. However, bridges also mean that more people will move in the other direction—seeing the beautiful park on the other side of the river and coming over to explore.

Who will those people be? Will they be like the people on the development corporation bus? Will they be white? Will they be Black? Will newcomers appreciate the beauty and the community? Will the growth allow the people who have been living here for generations to remain safely in place, or will the newcomers crossing the new bridges send away the people who have been here all along?

There isn't a way to stop the creation of the bridges, and at any rate, they are needed. In the face of this reality, city leaders and residents alike ask themselves how to preserve this stronghold of culture and maintain this last bastion against the forces that drive change in the remainder of the city.

What the voices from the eastern side of the river say in answer is straightforward. The answer to these questions is to listen to the claims that the community has already made. The answer is not to look away from the racial effects of urban change but to confront them head-on. The answer is to reposition outsiders' characterization of the neighborhood. The answer is to keep the neighborhood's Black culture at its core. The answer is to listen to the Black side of the river.

### Notes

1. The Anacostia Park celebrated its centennial in 2020, during the production of this volume.
2. Bonilla-Silva, *Racism without Racists*.

3. Robinson, *Disintegration.*

4. NAACP is the National Association for the Advancement of Colored People. I call President Obama "Black" here because he fits into Robinson's system of the fourth group of Black people—Emergent Blacks—which includes individuals of mixed race.

5. Williams and Emamdjomeh, "America Is More Diverse than Ever—But Still Segregated," *The Washington Post,* May 10, 2018.

6. Coates, "Case for Reparations." Coates provides a particularly lucid explanation of the roots of housing segregation and resultant property value differences in this longform article.

7. Pattillo, *Black on the Block.*

8. Prince, *African Americans and Gentrification;* Modan, *Turf Wars,* chap. 5.

9. Scollon and Scollon, *Discourses in Place.*

10. Prince, *African Americans and Gentrification,* 105.

11. Flipping refers to the practice of buying a house in a depressed market and selling it within a short period of time (usually within a year) at a higher price.

12. Rabinowitz, "What Are the District's Most House-Flipped Neighborhoods?"

13. Wilkerson, *Warmth of Other Suns.* Wilkerson talks about how Washington, though south of the Mason-Dixon Line, always held a position in the minds of Southern Blacks as being the "North" because it was the capital of the Union.

14. Wolfram, "Sociolinguistic Myths" and "Sociolinguistic Construction."

15. Kurath et al., *Linguistic Atlas of New England*; Kurath and McDavid, *Pronunciation of English;* Kretzschmar et al., *Handbook.*

16. Labov, *Language in the Inner City.* In Labov's New York fieldwork, where AAL is in contact with non-rhotic white varieties, speakers show more variability in rhoticity in AAL than those in Wolfram's contemporaneous work in Detroit, where the local white variety is largely r-full. See Wolfram, "Sociolinguistic Myths," for further discussion.

17. Gooden, "Authentically Black"; Bloomquist, "Dialect Differences."

18. Rickford, "African American Vernacular English in California."

19. Bailey and Cukor-Avila, "Rural Texas."

20. Hinton and Pollock, "Regional Variations."

21. Labov, *Social Stratification;* Becker, "/R/ and the Constructions of Place Identity"; Coggshall and Becker, "Vowel Phonologies."

22. Shuy, Wolfram, and Riley, *Field Techniques*; Wolfram, "Sociolinguis-

tic Construction"; Quartey and Schilling, "Shaping 'Connected'"; Grieser, "Language of Professional Blackness"; Lee, "Phonetic Variation" and "Discourse on Southeast's Bad Reputation"; Nylund, "Phonological Variation"; Holliday, "Intonational Variation."

23. Kendall and Farrington, "Corpus of Regional African American Language."

24. See Preston, "Language with an Attitude," for examples.

25. Rosa, *Looking like a Language*, 2.

26. Crenshaw, "Mapping the Margins"; Delgado and Stefancic, *Critical Race Theory*.

27. Pattillo, *Black on the Block*.

28. Lakoff and Johnson, *Metaphors We Live By*.

29. Hutchinson, *Anacostia Story*.

# References

Alim, H. Samy. *You Know My Steez: An Ethnographic and Sociolinguistic Study of Styleshifting in a Black American Speech Community.* Publication of the American Dialect Society. Durham, NC: Duke University Press, 2004.

Alim, H. Samy, John R. Rickford, and Arnetha F. Ball, eds. *Raciolinguistics: How Language Shapes Our Ideas about Race.* New York: Oxford University Press, 2016.

Alim, H. Samy, and Geneva Smitherman. *Articulate while Black.* Oxford: Oxford University Press, 2012.

Alpert, David. "DC Has Almost No White Residents without College Degrees. (It's a Different Story for Black Residents.)" *Greater Greater Washington* blog, 2016, https://ggwash.org/view/42563/dc-has-almost-no-white-residents-without-college-degrees-its-a-different-story-for-black-residents.

Amos, Alcione M. "Ten Strong: Women of Barry Farm/Hillsdale." Lecture at Anacostia Branch Library, Washington, DC, August 5, 2019.

Anacostia Library. https://www.dclibrary.org/node/579.

Anacostia Waterfront Trust. "The Anacostia in History: October 15, 2015." https://www.anacostiatrust.org/anacostia-trust/2015/10/15/the-anacostia-in-history. Accessed August 15, 2019.

Anderson, Kate T. "Justifying Race Talk: Indexicality and the Social Construction of Race and Linguistic Value." *Journal of Linguistic Anthropology* 18, no. 1 (2008): 108–29.

Bailey, Guy, and Patricia Cukor-Avila. "Rural Texas African American English." In *The Oxford Handbook of African American Language*, edited by Sonja Lanehart, 181–200. Oxford: Oxford University Press, 2015.

Baker-Bell, April. *Linguistic Justice: Black Language, Literacy, Identity, and Pedagogy.* Oxfordshire: Routledge, 2020.

Baugh, John. *Beyond Ebonics: Linguistic Pride and Racial Prejudice.* Oxford: Oxford University Press, 2000.

———. "A Dissection of Style-Shifting." In *Style and Sociolinguistic Variation*, edited by John R. Rickford and Penelope Eckert, 109–18. Cambridge: Cambridge University Press, 2012.

———. "The Politicization of Changing Terms of Self-Reference among American Slave Descendants." *American Speech* 66, no. 2 (Summer 1991): 133–46.

Becker, Kara. "/R/ and the Construction of Place Identity on New York City's Lower East Side." *Journal of Sociolinguistics* 13, no. 5 (2009): 634–58.

———. "The Sociolinguistic Interview." In *Data Collection in Sociolinguistics: Methods and Applications*, edited by Christine Mallinson, Becky Childs, and Gerard Van Herk, 91–100. New York: Routledge, 2013.

Bell, Allan. "Back in Style: Reworking Audience Design." In *Style and Sociolinguistic Variation*, edited by Penelope Eckert and John R. Rickford, 139–69. Cambridge: Cambridge University Press, 2012.

———. "Language Style as Audience Design." *Language in Society* 13, no. 2 (1984): 145–204. http://journals.cambridge.org/action/displayAbstract?fromPage=online&aid=2990984.

Bernstein Management Corporation. "1600 Pennsylvania Avenue." https://www.bmcproperties.com/live/washington-dc/capitol-hill/1600-pennsylvania-avenue-se-apartments. Accessed August 15, 2019.

Bloomquist, Jennifer. "Dialect Differences in Central Pennsylvania: Regional Dialect Use and Adaptation by African Americans in the Lower Susquehanna Valley." *American Speech* 84, no. 1 (2009): 27–47.

Bonilla-Silva, Eduardo. *Racism without Racists: Color-Blind Racism and the Persistence of Racial Inequality in the United States*. Washington, DC: Rowman & Littlefield, 2006.

Britt, Erica, and Tracey Weldon. "African American English in the Middle Class." In *Oxford Handbook of African American Language*, edited by Sonja L. Lanehart, 800–816. Oxford: Oxford University Press, 2015.

Bucholtz, Mary. "Sociolinguistic Nostalgia and the Authentication of Identity." *Journal of Sociolinguistics* 7, no. 3 (2003): 398–416.

———. "'Why Be Normal?': Language and Identity Practices in a Community of Nerd Girls." *Language in Society* 28, no. 2 (1999): 203–23.

Building Bridges across the River. https://bbardc.org/. Accessed December 9, 2019.

Campbell-Kibler, Kathryn. "Accent, (ING), and the Social Logic of Listener Perceptions." *American Speech* 82, no. 1 (2007): 32–64.

———. "I'll Be the Judge of That: Diversity in Social Perceptions of (Ing)." *Language in Society* 37, no. 5 (2008): 637–59.

Casselman, Amos B. "The Virginia Portion of the District of Columbia." *Records of the Columbia Historical Society, Washington, D.C.* 12 (1909): 115–41.

Chafe, Wallace. *Discourse, Consciousness, and Time: The Flow and Displacement of Conscious Experience in Speaking and Writing.* Chicago: University of Chicago Press, 1994.

Charity Hudley, Anne H., and Christine Mallinson. *Understanding English Language Variation in U.S. Schools.* Multicultural Education Series. New York: Teachers College Press, 2010.

———. *We Do Language: English Language Variation in the Secondary English Classroom.* New York: Teachers College Press, 2014.

City of Washington, DC. "Advisory Neighborhood Commissions." https://anc.dc.gov/page/about-ancs.

———. "DC's Economic Strategy." https://dceconomicstrategy.com.

Coates, Ta-Nehisi. "The Case for Reparations." *Atlantic* 313, no. 5 (2014): 54–71.

Coggshall, E. L., and K. Becker. "The Vowel Phonologies of African American and White New York City Residents." In *African American English Speakers and Their Participation in Local Sound Changes: A Comparative Study,* edited by Erik Thomas and Malcah Yaeger-Dror, 101–28. *Publication of the American Dialect Society* 94, no. 1 (2009).

Craig, Holly K., and Julie A. Washington. "Grade-Related Changes in the Production of African American English." *Journal of Speech, Language & Hearing Research* 47, no. 2 (2004): 450–63.

———. *Malik Goes to School: Examining the Language Skills of African American Students from Preschool–5th Grade.* London: Psychology Press, 2005.

Crenshaw, Kimberlé. "Mapping the Margins: Intersectionality, Identity Politics, and Violence against Women of Color." *Stanford Law Review* 43, no. 6 (1991): 1241–99. https://doi.org/10.2307/1229039. http://www.jstor.org/stable/1229039.

Cukor-Avila, Patricia. "Co-Existing Grammars: The Relationship between the Evolution of African American and Southern White Vernacular English in the South." In *Sociocultural and Historical Contexts of African American English,* edited by Sonja L. Lanehart, 93–128. Amsterdam: John Benjamins, 2001.

Dale, Dianne. *The Village That Shaped Us.* Self-published, 2011.

DeBose, Charles E. "African American Church Language." In *The Oxford Handbook of African American Language,* edited by Sonja Lanehart, 371–86. Oxford: Oxford University Press, 2015.

Delfino, Jennifer B. "Fighting Words? Joning as Conflict Talk and Identity Performance among African American Preadolescents." *Journal of Sociolinguistics* 20, no. 5 (2016): 631–53.

———. *Speaking of Race: Language, Identity, and Schooling among African American Children*. Lanham, MD: Lexington, 2020.

Delgado, Richard, and Jean Stefancic. *Critical Race Theory: An Introduction*. New York: New York University Press, 2017.

*Dictionary of American Regional English*. www.daredictionary.com.

District of Columbia. *Inclusionary Zoning Fiscal Year 2018 Annual Report*. Washington, DC: 2018. https://dhcd.dc.gov/page/fy2018-inclusionary-zoning-annual-report.

———. Open Data DC. https://opendata.dc.gov/.

District of Columbia, Washington Metropolitan Area Transit. *District of Columbia Transit Alternatives Analysis*. Washington, DC: Department of Transportation, 2005.

District of Columbia Planning Office. DC State Data Visualization Portal. https://dcdataviz.dc.gov/.

Du Bois, John W. "The Stance Triangle." In *Stancetaking in Discourse: Subjectivity, Evaluation, Interaction*, edited by Robert Englebretson, 139–82. Amsterdam, Netherlands: John Benjamins, 2007.

Eckert, Penelope. "Style and Social Meaning." In *Style and Sociolinguistic Variation*, edited by John R. Rickford and Penelope Eckert, 119–26. Cambridge: Cambridge University Press, 2001.

———. "Variation and the Indexical Field." *Journal of Sociolinguistics* 12, no. 4 (2008): 453–76.

Eckert, Penelope, and Sally McConnell-Ginet. "Communities of Practice: Where Language, Gender, and Power All Live." In *Locating Power: Proceedings of the 1992 Berkeley Women and Language Conference*, 89–99. Berkeley, CA: Berkeley Women and Language Group, 1992.

Eckert, Penelope, and John R. Rickford, eds. *Style and Sociolinguistic Variation*. Cambridge: Cambridge University Press, 2002.

Fairclough, Norman. *Discourse and Social Change*. Vol. 10. Cambridge: Polity, 1992.

Fasold, Ralph W. *Tense Marking in Black English: A Linguistic and Social Analysis*. Fort Worth, TX: Harcourt College, 1972.

Fitzpatrick, Sandra, and Maria R. Goodwin. *The Guide to Black Washington: Places and Events of Historical and Cultural Significance in the Nation's Capital*. New York: Hippocrene, 2001.

Flores, Nelson, and Jonathan Rosa. "Undoing Appropriateness: Raciolinguistic Ideologies and Language Diversity in Education." *Harvard Educational Review* 85, no. 2 (2015): 149–71.

Gale, Dennis E. *Washington, D.C.: Inner-City Revitalization and Minority Suburbanization.* Philadelphia: Temple University Press, 1987.

Gee, James Paul. *An Introduction to Discourse Analysis: Theory and Method.* Milton Park, Oxfordshire: Routledge, 2014.

———. *Social Linguistics and Literacies: Ideology in Discourses.* Milton Park, Oxfordshire: Routledge, 2015.

Goffman, Erving. *Frame Analysis: An Essay on the Organization of Experience.* Cambridge, MA: Harvard University Press, 1974.

———. "The Presentation of Self in Everyday Life [1959]." *Contemporary Sociological Theory* (2002): 46–61.

Gooden, Shelome. "Authentically Black, Bona Fide Pittsburgher: A First Look at Intonation in African American Women's Language in Pittsburgh." In *African American Women's Language: Discourse, Education and Identity*, edited by Sonja Lanehart, 142–64. Newcastle upon Tyne, UK: Cambridge Scholars, 2009.

Graham, Lawrence Otis. *Our Kind of People: Inside America's Black Upper Class.* New York: Harper Perennial, 1999.

Green, Lisa J. *African American English: A Linguistic Introduction.* Cambridge: Cambridge University Press, 2002.

———. *Language and the African American Child.* Cambridge: Cambridge University Press, 2010.

Gregory, James N. *The Southern Diaspora: How the Great Migrations of Black and White Southerners Transformed America.* Chapel Hill: University of North Carolina Press, 2006.

Grieser, Jessica. "Critical Race Theory and the New Sociolinguistics." In *Crossing Borders, Making Connections: Interdisciplinarity in Linguistics*, edited by Allison Burkette and Tamara Worhol, 41–58. Berlin: De Gruyter, 2021.

———. "Investigating Topic-Based Style Shifting in the Classic Sociolinguistic Interview." *American Speech* 94, no. 1 (2019): 54–71.

———. "The Language of Professional Blackness: African American English at the Intersection of Race, Place, and Class in Southeast, Washington, D.C." PhD dissertation, Georgetown University, 2015.

———. "Locating Style: Style-Shifting to Characterize Community at the Border of Washington, D.C." *University of Pennsylvania Working Papers in Linguistics* 19, no. 2 (2013).

———. "Two Sides of the Style Coin: Matching Morphosyntactic and Phonological Variation in Middle Class African American English." Paper presented at New Ways of Analyzing Variation Conference 46, Madison, Wisconsin, October 2017.

Gumperz, John Joseph. *Discourse Strategies*. Vol. 1. Cambridge: Cambridge University Press, 1982.

———. "The Speech Community." In *Linguistic Anthropology: A Reader*, edited by Alessandro Duranti, 68–73. Hoboken, NJ: Wiley, 2009.

Gutheim, Frederick, and Antoinette J. Lee. *Worthy of the Nation: Washington, DC, from L'enfant to the National Capital Planning Commission*. Baltimore: Johns Hopkins University Press, 2006.

Hackworth, Jason, and Neil Smith. "The Changing State of Gentrification." *Tijdschrift voor economische en sociale geografie* 92, no. 4 (2001): 464–77.

Harré, Rom, and Fathali M. Moghaddam. *The Self and Others: Positioning Individuals and Groups in Personal, Political, and Cultural Contexts*. Westport, CT: Greenwood, 2003.

Harré, Rom, and Luk Van Langenhove. *Positioning Theory: Moral Contexts of International Action*. Hoboken, NJ: Wiley-Blackwell, 1998.

Hinton, Linette N., and Karen E. Pollock. "Regional Variations in the Phonological Characteristics of African American Vernacular English." *World Englishes* 19, no. 1 (2000): 59–71.

Hoffman, M. F., and J. A. Walker. "Ethnolects and the City: Ethnic Orientation and Linguistic Variation in Toronto English." *Language Variation and Change* 22, no. 1 (2010): 37–67. http://journals.cambridge.org/action/displayAbstract?fromPage=online&aid=7737152.

Holliday, Nicole. "Intonational Variation, Linguistic Style, and the Black/Biracial Experience." PhD dissertation, New York University, 2016.

———. "Multiracial Identity and Racial Complexity in Sociolinguistic Variation." *Language and Linguistics Compass* 13, no. 8 (2019): e12345.

Hoover, Mary Rhodes. "Community Attitudes toward Black English." *Language in Society* 7, no. 1 (1978): 65–87.

Hunter, Marcus Anthony, and Zandria Robinson. *Chocolate Cities: The Black Map of American Life*. Berkeley: University of California Press, 2018.

Hutchinson, Louise Daniel. *The Anacostia Story, 1608–1930*. Washington, DC: Smithsonian Institution Press, 1977.

Hymes, Dell. "Speech Community." In *Linguistic Anthropology: A Reader*, edited by Alessandro Duranti, 74–94. Hoboken, NJ: Wiley, 2001.

Irvine, Judith T., and Susan Gal. "Language Ideology and Linguistic Differentiation." In *Linguistic Anthropology: A Reader*, 2nd ed., edited by Alessandro Duranti, 35–83. Hoboken, NJ: Wiley-Blackwell, 2009.

Jaffe, Harry. *Dream City: Race, Power, and the Decline of Washington*. New York: Simon & Schuster, 1994.

JDLand.com: Near Southeast DC Redevelopment. "The Harlow/Square 769n." https://www.jdland.com/dc/harlow.cfm.

Johnstone, Barbara. "Community and Contest: Midwestern Men and Women Creating Their Worlds in Conversational Storytelling." In *Gender and Conversational Interaction*, edited by Deborah Tannen, 62–80. Oxford: Oxford University Press, 1993.

———. "Stance, Style, and the Linguistic Individual." In *Stance: Sociolinguistic Perspectives*, edited by Alexandra Jaffe, 29–52. Oxford: Oxford University Press, 2009.

Kärkkäinen, Elise. *Epistemic Stance in English Conversation: A Description of Its Interactional Functions, with a Focus on* I Think. Amsterdam, Netherlands: John Benjamins, 2003.

Kendall, Tyler, and Charlie Farrington. "The Corpus of Regional African American Language. Version (CORAAL) 2018.04.06." The Online Resources for African American Language Project, 2018. http://oraal.uoregon.edu/coraal.

Kiesling, Scott Fabius. "Men's Identities and Sociolinguistic Variation: The Case of Fraternity Men." *Journal of Sociolinguistics* 2, no. 1 (1998): 69–99.

Kirkland, David. "Black Masculine Language." In *The Oxford Handbook of African American Language*, edited by Sonja Lanehart, 834–49. Oxford: Oxford University Press, 2015.

Kohn, Mary, Walt Wolfram, Charlie Farrington, Jennifer Renn, and Janneke Van Hofwegen. *African American Language: Language Development from Infancy to Adulthood*. Cambridge: Cambridge University Press, 2020.

Kretzschmar, William A., Jr., Virginia G. McDavid, Theodore K. Lerud, and Ellen Johnson, eds. *Handbook of the Linguistic Atlas of the Middle and South Atlantic States*. Chicago: University of Chicago Press, 1993.

Kurath, Hans, Bernard Bloch, Marcus Lee Hansen, and Julia Bloch, eds. *Linguistic Atlas of New England: Handbook of the Linguistic Geography of New England*. Providence, RI: Brown University Press, 1939.

Kurath, Hans, and Raven A. McDavid. *The Pronunciation of English in the Atlantic States*. Ann Arbor: University of Michigan Press, 1961.

Labov, William. "The Anatomy of Style-Shifting." In *Style and Sociolin-*

*guistic Variation*, edited by Penelope Eckert and John Rickford, 85–108. Cambridge: Cambridge University Press, 2012.

———. "Contraction, Deletion, and Inherent Variability of the English Copula." *Language* 45, no. 4 (1969): 715–62.

———. "Field Methods of the Project on Linguistic Change and Variation." In *Language in Use: Readings in Sociolinguistics*, edited by John Baugh and Joel Sherzer, 28–53. Englewood Cliffs, NJ: Prentice Hall, 1984.

———. *Language in the Inner City*. Philadelphia: University of Pennsylvania Press, 1972.

———. *The Social Stratification of English in New York City*. Cambridge: Cambridge University Press, 1966.

Labov, William, Sharon Ash, Maya Ravindranath, Tracey Weldon, Maciej Baranowski, and Naomi Nagy. "Properties of the Sociolinguistic Monitor." *Journal of Sociolinguistics* 15, no. 4 (2011): 431–63.

Lakoff, George. *The All New Don't Think of an Elephant! Know Your Values and Frame the Debate*. Hartford, VT: Chelsea Green, 2014.

Lakoff, George, and Mark Johnson. *Metaphors We Live By*. Chicago: University of Chicago Press, 1980.

Lanehart, Sonja L. *African American Women's Language: Discourse, Education, and Identity*. Newcastle upon Tyne, UK: Cambridge Scholars, 2009.

Lanehart, Sonja L., ed. *The Oxford Handbook of African American Language*. Oxford: Oxford University Press, 2015.

Lave, Jean, and Etienne Wenger. *Situated Learning: Legitimate Peripheral Participation*. Cambridge: Cambridge University Press, 1991.

Lee, Sinae. "Discourse on Southeast's Bad Reputation: Positioning of African Americans in Washington, DC." *Discourse & Society* 29, no. 4 (2018): 420–35.

———. "Phonetic Variation in Washington DC: Race, Neighborhood, and Gender." PhD dissertation, Georgetown University, 2016.

Lou, Jackie Jia. *The Linguistic Landscape of Chinatown: A Sociolinguistic Ethnography*. Clevedon, UK: Multilingual Matters, 2016.

Macaulay, Ronald. "The Question of Genre." In *Style and Sociolinguistic Variation*, edited by John Rickford and Penelope Eckert, 78–82. Cambridge: Cambridge University Press, 2012.

Mitchell-Kernan, Claudia. "Signifying and Marking: Two Afro-American Speech Acts." In *Linguistic Anthropology: A Reader*, edited by Alessandro Duranti, 151–64. Hoboken, NJ: Wiley, 2009.

———. "Signifying, Loud-Talking and Marking." In *Rappin'and Stylin' Out: Communication in Urban Black America*, edited by Thomas Kochman, 315–35. Urbana: University of Illinois Press, 1972.

Modan, Gabriella Gahlia. *Turf Wars: Discourse, Diversity, and the Politics of Place*. Hoboken, NJ: Wiley-Blackwell, 2007.

Morgan, Marcyliena. "The African American Speech Community." In *Linguistic Anthropology: A Reader*, edited by Alessandro Duranti, 74–94. Hoboken, NJ: Wiley, 2001.

———. "African American Women's Language: Mother Tongues United." In *The Oxford Handbook of African American Language*, edited by Sonja Lanehart, 817–33. Oxford: Oxford University Press, 2015.

Muller, John. *Frederick Douglass in Washington, D.C.: The Lion of Anacostia*. Mount Pleasant, SC: Arcadia, 2012.

National Park Service. "The L'Enfant and Mcmillan Plans." https://www.nps.gov/nr/travel/wash/lenfant.htm. Accessed August 15, 2019.

National Underground Railroad Freedom Center. "About Us." https://www.freedomcenter.org/about-us. Accessed March 4, 2019.

New Communities Initiative. "Barry Farm Redevelopment Plan." http://dcnewcommunities.org/barry-farm-development/http://dcnewcommunities.org/barry-farm-development/. Accessed August 15, 2019.

Nylund, Anastasia. "Phonological Variation at the Intersection of Ethnoracial Identity, Place, and Style in Washington, D.C." PhD dissertation, Georgetown University, 2013.

Open Data DC. "Demographic ACS Characteristics 2011 to 2015." Opendata.dc.gov. Accessed August 2021. https://opendata.dc.gov/datasets/demographic-acs-characteristics-2011-to-2015.

Palen, J. John, and Bruce London. *Gentrification, Displacement, and Neighborhood Revitalization*. Albany: SUNY Press, 1984.

Paris, Django. *Language across Difference: Ethnicity, Communication, and Youth Identities in Changing Urban Schools*. Cambridge: Cambridge University Press, 2011.

Pattillo, Mary. "Black on the Block." In *Racial Structure and Radical Politics in the African Diaspora*, edited by James L. Conyers Jr., 21–52. Milton Park, Oxfordshire: Routledge, 2017.

———. *Black on the Block: The Politics of Race and Class in the City*. Chicago: University of Chicago Press, 2007.

———. *Black Picket Fences: Privilege and Peril among the Black Middle Class*. Chicago: University of Chicago Press, 2013.

Podesva, Robert. "Phonation Type as a Stylistic Variable: The Use of Falsetto in Constructing a Persona." *Journal of Sociolinguistics* 11, no. 4 (2007): 478–504.

———. "Salience and the Social Meaning of Declarative Contours." *Journal of English Linguistics* 39, no. 3 (2011): 233–64. http://eng.sagepub.com /content/39/3/233.short.

———. "Stance as a Window into the Race-Language Connection: Evidence from African American and White Speakers in Washington, D.C." In *Raciolinguistics: How Language Shapes Our Ideas about Race*, edited by H. Samy Alim, John R. Rickford, and Arnetha F. Ball, 203–20. New York: Oxford University Press, 2016.

Preservation of Affordable Housing (POAH). Barry Farm. https://www.poah .org/property/district-columbia/barry-farm. Accessed February 15, 2019.

Preston, Dennis. "Language with an Attitude." In *The Handbook of Language Variation and Change*, edited by J. K. Chambers and Natalie Schilling, 157–82. Hoboken, NJ: Wiley, 2018.

Prince, Sabiyha. *African Americans and Gentrification in Washington, DC: Race, Class and Social Justice in the Nation's Capital.* Milton Park, Oxfordshire: Routledge, 2016.

———. *Constructing Belonging: Class, Race, and Harlem's Professional Workers.* Milton Park, Oxfordshire: Routledge, 2004.

Quartey, Minnie, and Natalie Schilling. "Shaping 'Connected' versus 'Disconnected' Identities in Narrative Discourse in DC African American Language." *American Speech* 94, no. 1 (2019): 131–47.

Rabinowitz, Kate. "What Are the District's Most House-Flipped Neighborhoods? D.C. Data." 2015, accessed November 10, 2017, https://www.data lensdc.com/dc-property-flipping.html.

Rahman, Jacqueline. "Middle-Class African Americans: Reactions and Attitudes toward African American English." *American Speech* 83, no. 2 (2008): 141–76. http://americanspeech.dukejournals.org/cgi/content /abstract/83/2/141.

Rampersad, Arnold. *The Life of Langston Hughes, 1902–1941: I, Too, Sing America.* Vol. 1. Oxford: Oxford University Press, 2001.

Renn, Jennifer, and J. Michael Terry. "Operationalizing Style: Quantifying the Use of Style Shift in the Speech of African American Adolescents." *American Speech* 84, no. 4 (2009): 367–90.

Rickford, John. *African American Vernacular English: Features, Evolution, Educational Implications.* Hoboken, NJ: Wiley-Blackwell, 1999. http:// www.amazon.com/dp/0631212450.

———. "African American Vernacular English in California: Over Four Decades of Vibrant Variationist Research." In *The Oxford Handbook of African American Language*, edited by Sonja Lanehart, 299–315. Oxford: Oxford University Press, 2015.

———. "Unequal Partnership: Sociolinguistics and the African American Speech Community." *Language in Society* 26, no. 2 (1997): 161–97.

Rickford, John R., Arnetha Ball, Renee Blake, Raina Jackson, and Nomi Martin. "Rappin on the Copula Coffin: Theoretical and Methodological Issues in the Analysis of Copula Variation in African-American Vernacular English." *Language Variation and Change* 3, no. 1 (1991): 103–32.

Rickford, John, and Faye McNair-Knox. "Addressee- and Topic-Influenced Style Shift: A Quantitative Sociolinguistic Study." In *Sociolinguistic Perspectives on Register*, edited by Douglas Biber and Edward Finegan, 235–76. Oxford: Oxford University Press, 1994.

Rickford, John, and Mackenzie Price. "Girlz II Women: Age-Grading, Language Change and Stylistic Variation." *Journal of Sociolinguistics* 17, no. 2 (2013): 143–79.

Rickford, John Russell, and Russell John Rickford. *Spoken Soul: The Story of Black English*. Malden, MA: Wiley, 2000.

Robinson, Eugene. *Disintegration: The Splintering of Black America*. New York: Doubleday, 2010.

Rosa, Jonathan. *Looking like a Language, Sounding like a Race: Raciolinguistic Ideologies and the Learning of Latinidad*. New York: Oxford University Press, 2019.

Sankoff, David, and Suzanne Laberge. "The Linguistic Market and the Statistical Explanation of Variability." *Linguistic Variation: Models and Methods* 239 (1978): 50.

Scollon, Ron, and Suzie Wong Scollon. *Discourses in Place: Language in the Material World*. Milton Park, Oxfordshire: Routledge, 2003.

Seymour, Harry N., Linda Bland-Stewart, and Lisa J. Green. "Difference versus Deficit in Child African American English." *Language, Speech, and Hearing Services in Schools* 29, no. 2 (1998): 96–108.

Shuy, Roger W., Walt Wolfram, and William K. Riley. *Field Techniques in an Urban Language Study*. Washington, DC: Center for Applied Linguistics, 1968.

Smith, Kathryn S. *Washington at Home: An Illustrated History of Neighborhoods in the Nation's Capital*. Baltimore: Johns Hopkins University Press, 2010.

Smith, Neil. "Gentrification and the Rent Gap." *Annals of the Association of*

*American Geographers* 77, no. 3 (1987): 462–65. https://doi.org/10.1111
/j.1467-8306.1987.tb00171.x.

———. *The New Urban Frontier: Gentrification and the Revanchist City.*
Sussex, UK: Psychology Press, 1996.

Smitherman, Geneva. *Talkin' That Talk: Language, Culture, and Education in African America.* Milton Park, Oxfordshire: Routledge, 2000.

———. "'What Is Africa to Me?': Language, Ideology, and African American." *American Speech* 66, no. 2 (1991): 115–32. https://doi.org/10.2307/455881.

Smithsonian Anacostia Community Museum and Center for African American History and Culture. *The Black Washingtonians: The Anacostia Museum Illustrated Chronology.* Hoboken, NJ: Wiley, 2005.

———. "The Making of a Museum." Washington, DC: Smithsonian Institution, 1968.

Spears, Arthur K. "African-American Language Use: Ideology and So-Called Obscenity." In *African-American English: Structure, History, and Use,* edited by Salikoko S. Mufwene, Guy Bailey, John Baugh, and John R. Rickford, 226–50. London: Routledge, 1998.

———. "African American Standard English." In *The Oxford Handbook of African American Language,* edited by Sonja Lanehart, 786–99. Oxford: Oxford University Press, 2015.

———. "Bare Nouns in African American English (AAE)." *Creole Language Library* 31 (2007): 421.

Strauss, Anselm, and Juliet M. Corbin. *Grounded Theory in Practice.* Thousand Oaks, CA: Sage, 1997.

Su, Yipeng, and Robin Wang. "Three Ways Bikeshare Can Be More Equitable in DC." *Greater Greater Washington,* July, 15, 2019, https://ggwash.org/view/70922/three-ways-bikeshare-can-help-counter-disparities-in-dc.

Tannen, Deborah. *Talking Voices: Repetition, Dialogue, and Imagery in Conversational Discourse.* Cambridge: Cambridge University Press, 2007.

———. "What's in a Frame? Surface Evidence for Underlying Expectations." In *Framing in Discourse,* edited by Deborah Tannen, 14–56. Oxford: Oxford University Press, 1993.

Taylor, Orlando L. "Response to 'Social Dialects and the Field of Speech.'" In *Sociolinguistic Theory, Materials, and Training Programs: Three Related Studies, Final Report,* edited by Roger W. Shuy, Irwin Feigenbaum, and Allene Grognet, 21. Washington, DC: Center for Applied Linguistics, 1971.

THEARC Theater. https://bbardc.org/project/thearc. Accessed December 9, 2019.

Thomas, Erik. "Phonological and Phonetic Characteristics of African American Vernacular English." *Language and Linguistics Compass* 1, no. 5 (2007): 450–75.

Trinch, Shonna, and Edward Snajdr. "What the Signs Say: Gentrification and the Disappearance of Capitalism without Distinction in Brooklyn." *Journal of Sociolinguistics* 21, no. 1 (2017): 64–89.

Trotter, J. W., and N. Painter. *The Great Migration in Historical Perspective: New Dimensions of Race, Class, and Gender.* Bloomington: Indiana University Press, 1991.

Trudgill, Peter. "Sex, Covert Prestige and Linguistic Change in the Urban British English of Norwich." *Language in Society* 1, no. 2 (1972): 179–95.

Urban Institute. "Greater DC: Our Vision for the Region." https://greaterdc.urban.org/. Accessed December 2020.

US Census Bureau. "ACS 5 Year Estimates 2016." Census.gov. Accessed August 2021.

US Congress. "An Act for Establishing the Temporary and Permanent Seat of the Government of the United States." Washington, DC, 1790. Library of Congress. https://www.loc.gov/resource/rbpe.21500600/?st=text.

Van Hofwegen, Janneke. "Apparent-Time Evolution of /L/ in One African American Community." *Language Variation and Change* 22, no. 3 (2010): 373–96.

Van Hofwegen, Janneke, and Walt Wolfram. "Coming of Age in African American English: A Longitudinal Study." *Journal of Sociolinguistics* 14, no. 4 (2010): 427–55.

———. "On the Utility of Composite Indices in Longitudinal Language Study: The Case of African American Language." In *Panel Studies of Variation and Change*, edited by Suzanne Evans Wagner and Isabelle Buchstaller, 89–114. New York: Routledge, 2017.

Weldon, Tracey. *Middle Class African American English.* Cambridge: Cambridge University Press, 2021.

———. "Middle Class African American Language: A Self-Study." Paper presented at New Ways of Analyzing Variation Conference 40, Washington, DC, October 28, 2011.

Wilkerson, Isabel. *The Warmth of Other Suns: The Epic Story of America's Great Migration.* New York: Random House Digital, 2010.

Woldoff, Rachael A. *White Flight/Black Flight: The Dynamics of Racial Change in an American Neighborhood.* Ithaca, NY: Cornell University Press, 2011.

Wolfram, Walt. "The Relationship of White Southern Speech to Vernacular Black English." *Language* 50, no. 3 (1974): 498–527. https://doi.org/10.2307/412221.

———. "The Sociolinguistic Construction of African American Language." In *The Oxford Handbook of African American Language*, edited by Sonja Lanehart, 338–52. Oxford: Oxford University Press, 2015.

———. *A Sociolinguistic Description of Detroit Negro Speech*. Washington, DC: Center for Applied Linguistics, 1969.

———. "Sociolinguistic Myths in the Study of African American English." *Language and Linguistics Compass* 2 (2007): 292–313.

Wolfson, Nessa. "Speech Events and Natural Speech: Some Implications for Sociolinguistic Methodology." *Language in Society* 5, no. 2 (1976): 189–209.

# Index

*Figures, notes, and tables are indicated by f, n, and t following the page number.*

# About the Author

Jessi Grieser is an associate professor of English linguistics in the Department of English at the University of Tennessee. She researches discourse analytic and variationist approaches to the linkages between language and race and place identities, with a side of discourse analysis of online speech, especially in fan communities. *The Black Side of the River* is her first book.